W9-AZJ-259

ALL
THINGS
NEW

Also by John Eldredge

The Sacred Romance (with Brent Curtis)

Walking with God

Wild at Heart

Waking the Dead

Epic

Knowing the Heart of God

Beautiful Outlaw

Free to Live

Captivating (with Stasi Eldredge)

Fathered by God

Love and War (with Stasi Eldredge)

Killing Lions (with Samuel Eldredge)

Moving Mountains

ALL THINGS NEW

HEAVEN, EARTH, AND THE RESTORATION OF EVERYTHING YOU LOVE

JOHN ELDREDGE

NELSON
BOOKS

An Imprint of Thomas Nelson

© 2017 by John Eldredge

All rights reserved. No portion of this book may be reproduced, stored in a retrieval system, or transmitted in any form or by any means—electronic, mechanical, photocopy, recording, scanning, or other—except for brief quotations in critical reviews or articles, without the prior written permission of the publisher.

Published in Nashville, Tennessee, by Nelson Books, an imprint of Thomas Nelson. Nelson Books and Thomas Nelson are registered trademarks of HarperCollins Christian Publishing, Inc.

Published in association with Yates & Yates, www.yates2.com.

Thomas Nelson titles may be purchased in bulk for educational, business, fund-raising, or sales promotional use. For information, please e-mail SpecialMarkets@ThomasNelson.com.

Unless otherwise noted, Scripture quotations are taken from the Holy Bible, New International Version®, NIV®. Copyright © 1973, 1978, 1984, 2011 by Biblica, Inc.® Used by permission of Zondervan. All rights reserved worldwide. www.zondervan.com. The "NIV" and "New International Version" are trademarks registered in the United States Patent and Trademark Office by Biblica, Inc.®

Scripture quotations marked KJV are from the King James Version. Public domain.

Scripture quotations marked THE MESSAGE are from *The Message*. Copyright © by Eugene H. Peterson 1993, 1994, 1995, 1996, 2000, 2001, 2002. Used by permission of Tyndale House Publishers, Inc.

Scripture quotations marked NASB are from New American Standard Bible®. Copyright © 1960, 1962, 1963, 1968, 1971, 1972, 1973, 1975, 1977, 1995 by The Lockman Foundation. Used by permission. (www.Lockman.org)

Scripture quotations marked NKJV are from the New King James Version®. © 1982 by Thomas Nelson. Used by permission. All rights reserved.

Scripture quotations marked NLT are from the Holy Bible, New Living Translation. © 1996, 2004, 2007, 2013, 2015 by Tyndale House Foundation. Used by permission of Tyndale House Publishers, Inc., Carol Stream, Illinois 60188. All rights reserved.

Scripture quotations marked RSV are from Revised Standard Version of the Bible. Copyright 1946, 1952, and 1971 National Council of the Churches of Christ in the United States of America. Used by permission. All rights reserved.

Any Internet addresses, phone numbers, or company or product information printed in this book are offered as a resource and are not intended in any way to be or to imply an endorsement by Thomas Nelson, nor does Thomas Nelson vouch for the existence, content, or services of these sites, phone numbers, companies, or products beyond the life of this book.

ISBN 978-0-7180-3799-4 (HC)
ISBN 978-1-4002-0752-7 (TP)
ISBN 978-0-7180-3800-7 (eBook)
ISBN 978-0-7180-9893-3 (IE)

Library of Congress Cataloging-in-Publication Data

Names: Eldredge, John, 1960- author.
Title: All things new : heaven, earth, and the restoration of everything you love / John Eldredge.
Description: Nashville : Thomas Nelson, 2017. | Includes bibliographical references.
Identifiers: LCCN 2017011696 | ISBN 9780718037994
Subjects: LCSH: Redemption. | Heaven--Christianity. | Paradise.
Classification: LCC BT775 .E38 2017 | DDC 234--dc23 LC record available at https://lccn.loc.gov/2017011696

Printed in the United States of America

18 19 20 21 LSC 10 9 8 7 6 5 4 3 2 1

*To Patrick and Craig—who joined the Great
Cloud during the writing of this book*

I thought you were dead! But then I thought I was dead myself. Is everything sad going to come untrue?

Sam Gamgee in *The Return of the King*

Contents

Introduction: A Breathtaking Promise   ix

Chapter 1   Is There a Hope That Really   1
              Overcomes All This?

Chapter 2   The Renewal of All Things   19

Chapter 3   Let Us Be Honest   41

Chapter 4   The New Earth   61

Chapter 5   Our Restoration   83

Chapter 6   When Every Story Is Told Rightly   105

Chapter 7   The Overthrow of Evil   129

Chapter 8   What Do We Actually *Do*?   151

Chapter 9   The Marriage of Heaven and Earth   173

Chapter 10 Grab Hold with Both Hands   195

Acknowledgments   213

About the Author   215

Notes   217

An Excerpt from Defiant Joy   225

A Breathtaking Promise

We could sure use some hope right now."

I was chatting with a friend last week about the things going on in our lives and in the world, when she said this. We were talking about our loss of a dear colleague, but also about how everyone we know seems to be facing some hard thing or other. My friend is normally a very buoyant woman whatever the circumstance. There was a pause in the conversation, and then she sighed and expressed her longing for some hope.

Yes, hope would be very timely right about now.

Though we are trying to put a bold face on things, the human race is not doing well at all. Take any of our vital signs—you'll see. The rate of antidepressant use has gone through the ceiling in the last twenty years; antidepressants have become the third most common prescription drug.[1] Now, I believe in medication. But I think it says something about us when depression is the *leading* cause of disability worldwide.[2] Suicide rates are also skyrocketing; depending on the country, it is the first or second leading cause of death among our young people. In 2012, during the war in Afghanistan, we lost more of our soldiers to suicide than we did to combat.[3]

We appear to be suffering a great crisis of hope. It's taking place loudly in politics and economies; it's taking place quietly in the hearts of millions at this moment.

By hope, I don't mean wishful thinking. I'm not talking about "holding a positive thought," as one friend calls it. When I speak of hope, I mean *the confident anticipation that goodness is coming.* A rock-solid expectation, something we can build our lives on. Not the delicate and fragile hopes most people are trying to get by with.

What would you say is the great hope of your life these days?

If it is anything at all worth talking about, Christianity is supposed to be the triumphant entry of an astonishing hope breaking into human history. A hope above and beyond all former hopes. An unbreakable, unquenchable hope. But I'll be honest—far too often what gets presented as the "hope" of Christianity feels more like a bait and switch. "We understand that you will eventually lose everything you love, that you have already lost so much. Everything you love and hold dear, every precious memory and place you will lose, but afterward you get to go to this New Place Up Above!" Like a game show, where you don't win the car or the European vacation, but you do get some luggage and the kitchen knives.

The world doesn't believe it. And there are good reasons why.

When you consider the pain, suffering, and heartbreak contained in one children's hospital, one refugee camp, one abusive home or war-torn village over the course of a single day, it's almost too much to bear. But then consider that multiplied out across the planet, over all the days in a year, then down through history. It would take a pretty wild, astonishing, and breathtaking hope to overcome the agony and trauma of this world.

How is God going to make it all right? How is he going to redeem all of the suffering and loss of this world . . . and in your own life?

Escapism isn't going to do it, no matter what religious version you choose. What about all your hopes and dreams? What about all your special places and memories, the things most dear to your heart? Is there no hope for any of that? What we ache for is redemption; what our heart cries out for is *restoration*.

And I have some stunning, breathtaking news for you: restoration is exactly what Jesus promised. Despite what you may have been told, he didn't focus our hopes on the great airlift to heaven. He promised "the renewal of all things," including the earth you love, every precious part of it, and your own story (Matthew 19:28). The climax of the entire

Bible takes place with these words: "I am making everything new!" (Revelation 21:5). A day of Great Restoration is coming. Not annihilation—*restoration*. That is the only hope powerful enough to be for us what God calls the anchor of the soul: "We have this hope as an anchor for the soul" (Hebrews 6:19).

How you envision your future impacts your current experience more than anything else. Children starting the long school year feel very differently about waking each morning than those who know summer vacation is just a few days away. The woman recently served divorce papers feels very differently about her life than the woman who wakes the day before her wedding. How we feel about our future has enormous consequences for our hearts now. If you knew that God was going to restore your life and everything you love any day, if you believed a great and glorious goodness was coming to you—not in a vague heaven, but right here on this earth— you would have a hope to see you through anything. You would have an anchor for your soul, "an unbreakable spiritual lifeline, reaching past all appearances right to the very presence of God" (Hebrews 6:19 THE MESSAGE).

I'll be frank—if everything is going wonderfully for you right now, and you have every reason to believe it's going to stay that way, this book probably isn't for you. But if you are wondering why your soul feels so unsettled, and what there really is to look forward to, if you are longing for a wild, astonishing hope that could be an anchor for your life, read on. You're going to be very glad you did.

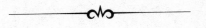

Picture a treasure chest.

Not a small box that might hold jewelry on a girl's night-stand—a large treasure chest, larger than any suitcase you own, larger than any suitcase you've ever seen.

Picture a massive oak treasure chest, like pirates might have used, with large iron hinges and a huge clasp. The size and age and strength of this strongbox say it was made for the most valuable things.

Inside this chest are all of the things you wish could some-how be restored to you. Everything you have lost, everything you know you will lose.

What fills your treasure chest?

CHAPTER 1

Is There a Hope That Really Overcomes All This?

It takes no courage to be an optimist, but it
takes a great deal of courage to have hope.

RABBI JONATHAN SACKS, *Celebrating Life*

The sunrise this morning was filled with such promise.

I was standing at the window in the early hours, praying, watching the dawn slowly bathe the hills in a golden light. The forest was utterly still, almost timeless. Each leaf was washed with a warm yellow glow, like candlelight; it covered the whole mountainside. Something about the bright, gentle beauty illuminating an entire forest made me feel that everything is going to be okay.

It is autumn now, and normally I'm not particularly happy

about that. I don't usually like the coming of fall because I know the long winter will soon descend with more darkness than light. The world will go into gray tones for too long. But this year I'm relieved to see the leaves turning pumpkin colors, the grasses fading into brown—earth shedding her beauty as she goes into hibernation. Because I just want this year to be over.

January began with a suicide in our extended family; I was the one to receive the phone call. I had to find my middle son and tell him his wife's dear brother took his tormented life. Then the two of us had to find her and break the news that would break her heart. Those were awful days.

A reprieve from the grief seemed to come a few months later, when both my oldest son and his wife and my grieving son and daughter-in-law came over one evening to tell Stasi and me we were going to become grandparents. Not just once, but twice, at the same time—both couples were expecting. They had T-shirts made for us; the shared happiness was simply wonderful. We talked about the cousins growing up together, little cowboys running around Gramma and Poppy's house bringing joy and lightheartedness. Maybe happiness gets the final word.

Then our oldest and his beloved wife went through a horrible, brutal miscarriage. I buried my first grandson on the mountain behind our home. We stood as a family around the tiny grave while his devastated mother spoke these words: "Patrick, the day we learned we were pregnant with you was the best day of our lives. And the day we lost you was the worst." Watching my children grieve is the worst thing I've gone through as a father.

But then promise rose again a few months later, as our attention was mercifully turned to the wedding of our youngest son. I love weddings; I love the beauty, the romance, all the fairy-tale symbolism. I love wedding *receptions*. Theirs was held outdoors under the stars of a summer night, with hanging lights and laughter and dancing. It seemed to whisper again that all will be well. There is something winsome and enchanting in the best wedding parties, something that speaks to the deepest longing in our hearts. No one wanted to leave.

We were all enjoying the afterglow the next morning when my phone rang. Our dear friend Craig, whom we've known for almost forty years, was calling to tell us his cancer had taken a terrible turn. A month earlier he was almost in remission; now he would die within six weeks. I hung up and threw my cell phone as far as I could. This would be the second time in my life I would lose my dearest, closest friend.

And that is why I am fine with the coming of fall, and the passing of this year.

Can we just be honest? Life is brutal.

There is just enough goodness to rouse our hearts with expectation, and plenty enough sadness to cut us back down. When the cutting down exceeds the rising up, you wonder if you shouldn't just stay down. "I wept when I was borne," wrote the Anglican poet George Herbert, "and every day shewes why."[1] Yes, life can also be beautiful. I am a lover of all the beautiful things in life. But may I point out that the movie by that name—*Life Is Beautiful*—takes place in a Nazi concentration camp. The story is precious in the way the father loves and protects his little boy from the ghoulish realities all around. But the father is killed at the end. Many, many people die horrible deaths at the end.

We need more than a silver-lining outlook on life. Much, much more. We need an unbreakable, unquenchable hope.

As I stood at the window for my morning vigil, the amber light of dawn was turning every fall color an even richer hue. It looked like something from a painting—transcendent, mythic. And for a moment it all felt brimming with promise. You've probably felt that promise too, as you stood in some favorite spot, watching the beauty of the rolling waves, marveling over spring flowers in the desert, walking the streets of Paris at night, sitting in your garden with a cup of coffee. Something keeps whispering to us through the beauty we love.

"Many things begin with seeing in this world of ours," wrote British artist Lilias Trotter. "There lies before us a beautiful, possible life."[2]

I savor those moments; they are among my most treasured memories. But whatever it is that speaks such promise, it seems to slip through our fingers every time we reach for it. I know that simply wanting this year to be over isn't the answer because who really knows what next year will bring? "Each day has enough trouble of its own," said the most compassionate man ever.[3]

WHAT ARE WE LOOKING FORWARD TO?

I keep checking my phone for e-mail and texts.

I do it all through the day; every alert gets my attention. I've been doing it for some time now. And the funny thing is, I'm not the kind of person who likes technology; I don't want to feel tied to my phone by an emotional umbilical cord. So what is this compulsion? What am I looking for? It's as though I'm looking for something.

And I'm not alone. People check their devices something like 110 times a day—one-third of their waking hours.[4] What is this obsession? I know we get a dopamine buzz when we receive a text, but something else is going on here.[5] After months and months of this obsession, I think I'm beginning to understand—the thing I keep looking for is good news. I am hoping for, looking for, longing for good news. We need to know that good is coming to us. We need to feel confident that a bright future is going to be given us and never taken away—not by anyone or anything.

I mentioned the global rise of depression and suicide; similar increases are happening with anxiety and various addictions.[6] Our search for happiness is getting desperate. Have you noticed all the hatred and rage? If you spend any time on social media you have. Perhaps you saw the fallout after the Cincinnati Zoo incident; it was hard not to. In May 2016, a three-year-old boy fell through the rails into the enclosure of a male gorilla at the zoo; the gorilla grabbed the boy and violently threw him around. The dangerous-animal response team shot the gorilla and saved the boy's life. A social media Chernobyl followed—vicious, venomous backlash against the zoo and the boy's parents. Hundreds of thousands of people called for the boy's parents to be prosecuted. I understand strong emotion, but we are talking full-blown *hatred* here. And it doesn't take much to provoke it.

Shortly after the zoo tragedy, the remake of the film *Ghostbusters* was released, with an all-female cast. I don't even begin to understand the poisonous response. Leslie Jones, an African American actress starring in the film, was bombarded online with "a stream of pornography, racist speech and hateful memes." She was compared to the gorilla shot at the zoo; she received photos with human semen on her face.[7] Over a *movie*?

Something is happening to the human heart. You need to understand what it is if you would make sense of any of this.

Human beings are by nature ravenous creatures; a famished craving haunts every one of us. We were created for utter happiness, joy, and life. But ever since we lost Eden, we have never known a day of total fullness; we are never filled in any lasting way. People are like cut flowers—we appear to be well, but we are severed from the vine. We are desperate, lustful creatures. We look to a marriage (or the hope of marriage), a child, our work, food, sex, alcohol, adventure, the next dinner out, the new car—anything to touch the ache inside us. We are *ravenous* beings.

And we have been untethered. Every institution that once

provided psychological and moral stability is crumbling—families, communities, church allegiances. We don't trust anyone or anything anymore; not our universities nor financial institutions, not religious hierarchies, and certainly not our political leaders. The breakdown adds a kind of unchecked desperation to our ravenous hunger.

Then the world stands in the way of our famished craving; it constantly thwarts us. People don't treat us as we long to be treated; we can't find the happiness we need. Our boss is harsh, so we sabotage him. Our spouse withholds sex, so we indulge online. The ravening won't be stopped. But boy, oh boy—when somebody gets in the way of our desperate hunger, they feel the fury of our rage. We are ready to kill. People shoot each other over traffic incidents. Parents abuse a baby who keeps them up at night. We vengefully crucify one another in social media.

This is our current condition—ravenous, psychologically untethered, increasingly desperate, ready to harm anything that gets in our way. And there appears to be nothing to stop the slide into chaos. "The falcon cannot hear the falconer," warned the poet W. B. Yeats in "The Second Coming":

> Things fall apart; the centre cannot hold;
> Mere anarchy is loosed upon the world.

Whatever else is at play here, we have clearly lost hope. We have no confident expectation that goodness is coming to us. When my friend said, "We could sure use some hope right now," she may have prophesied the final word over the human race.

LOOKING FOR A STRONGER HOPE

Scripture names hope as one of the Three Great Forces of human existence:

> Three things will last forever—faith, hope, and love.
>
> (1 CORINTHIANS 13:13 NLT)

By saying they last forever, God names these three as immortal powers. A life without faith has no meaning; a life without love isn't worth living; a life without hope is a dark cavern from which you cannot escape. These things aren't simply "virtues." Faith, hope, and love are mighty *forces* meant to carry your life forward, upward; they are your wings and the strength to use them.

I believe hope plays the critical role. You'll find it pretty hard to love when you've lost hope; hopelessness collapses into *who cares?* And what does it matter that we have faith if we have no hope? Faith is just a rigid doctrine with nothing to look forward to. Hope is the wind in your sails, the spring in your step. Hope is so essential to your being that Scripture calls it "an anchor for the soul" (Hebrews 6:19).

In an untethered world, we need a hope that can anchor us.

Those who are fighting cancer—or any physical affliction—will tell you that hope is essential if you would overcome. Abandon hope, and your body seems to give up the fight. Anyone who has walked the painful road of divorce knows that hope is the lifeline of a marriage; give up on hope and there is no reason to put in the hard work of staying together. People who lose hope are less likely to survive plane crashes and other survival scenarios. Hope is a determining factor in overcoming poverty. Hope literally heals the structures of your brain.[8]

But to really grasp hope's beauty and power, you only need to think of what it is like to lose all hope whatsoever. I shudder; my moments of hopelessness are the darkest memories of my life. When we lose hope we wander too close to the shadowlands of hell, whose occupants "every hope resign," according to Dante.[9] Hope is the sunlight of the soul; without it, our inner world walks about in shadows. But like a sunrise in the heart, hope sheds light over our view of everything else, casting all things in a new light. It wasn't merely sunlight bathing the mountain this morning—it was *hope*.

Faith is something that looks backward—we remember the ways God has come through for his people, and for us, and our belief is strengthened that he will come through again. Love is exercised in the present moment; we love in the "now." Hope is unique; hope looks forward, anticipating the good that is coming. Hope reaches into the future to take hold of something we do not yet have, may not yet even see.

———

Strong hope seizes the future that is not yet; it is the *confident expectation of goodness coming to us.*

It might be helpful to pause and ask yourself, *How is my hope these days? Where is my hope these days?*

THE ANSWER TO THE RIDDLE OF THE PROMISE

Optimism is not going to cut it. Trying to look on the bright side isn't going to sustain us through days like we are living in. Given how critical hope is to our lives, the most urgent question has to be, "Where is the hope that can overcome all the heartache of this world?"

"We all feel the riddle of the earth," wrote G. K. Chesterton. "The mystery of life is the plainest part of it. The clouds and curtains of darkness, the confounding vapours, these are the daily weather of this world."[10] Thank you, Gilbert; I love it when someone says perfectly what we've always known to be true but never named for ourselves. I think the mystery boils down to this:

Some sort of promise seems to be woven into the tapestry of life. It comes to us through golden moments, through beauty that takes our breath away, through precious memories and the hope even a birthday or vacation can awaken. It comes especially through the earth itself.

That promise fits perfectly with the deepest longing of our hearts—the longing for life to come together as we somehow know it was always meant to. The whispers of this promise touch a wild hope deep within our hearts, a hope we hardly dare to name.

Does it ever come true?

That's the mystery; that is the riddle. So let's start right here. Perhaps we can pick up the trail from here.

Now, this may sound a little odd for a man to admit, but I feel a sort of compassion for Imelda's shoe fetish.

For those of you who missed the scandal back in the '80s, Imelda Marcos was married to Ferdinand, former president of the Philippines. They were ousted from power in '86 and fled the country, leaving behind a fascinating treasure: designer shoes. Thousands and thousands of them. Like so many fellow dictators, the Marcoses lived an extravagant lifestyle—bankrolled by the state, of course—while their people went about barefoot in the streets. Thus the ousting. Imelda was rumored to have a thing for shoes, but truth again proved stranger than fiction. Her personal collection contained from 1,060 to 7,500 pairs.[11]

Think of it—acres and acres of gorgeous, dazzling shoes from the best salons in the world. If you wore then tossed a new pair every single day for ten years, you still couldn't wear them all.

What compels a person to obsessively hoard beauty they can never hope to see, let alone use in any meaningful way?

The media crucified Imelda, but I found the discovery fascinating. Fetishes are illuminating; they are a sort of peephole into the wild mystery of the human heart. We can hide our weirdness under a social disguise, we can maintain a good show, but our fetishes and fantasies blow our cover. The addict's ravenous hunger is there for all the world to see. Honestly—I felt a kind of empathy for Imelda, though I wouldn't go public with it till now. I think she was looking for the Ruby Slippers; she was looking for Somewhere Over the Rainbow. (This isn't so strange: after all, one shoe changed Cinderella's life.)

Imelda Marcos was looking for the kingdom of God.

I'll let you in on a little secret: your heart is made for the kingdom of God. This might be the most important thing anyone will ever tell you about yourself: your heart only thrives in one habitat, and that safe place is called the kingdom of God. Stay with me now.

THE RENEWAL OF ALL THINGS

Jesus Christ gave his life to give each of us a hope above and beyond all former hopes. Every action and teaching of his brilliant life were very intentionally directed at unveiling this hope to us. Late in the gospel of Matthew he described it with breathtaking clarity:

> "Truly I tell you, at the renewal of all things, when the Son of Man sits on his glorious throne . . . everyone who has left houses or brothers or sisters or father or mother or wife or children or fields for my sake will receive a hundred times as much and will inherit eternal life." (19:28–29)

At the renewal of all things?! God's intention for us is *the renewal of all things*? This is what the Son of God said; that is how he plainly described it. I can hardly speak. *Really?*

The Greek word used here for "renewal" is *palingenesia*, which is derived from two root words: *paling*, meaning "again," and *genesia*, meaning "beginning," which of course hearkens back to Genesis. Genesis again. Eden restored. Could it possibly be? Sometimes comparing the work of various translators gets us even closer to the meaning of a passage; let's look at two more:

> Jesus replied, "Yes, you have followed me. In the re-creation of the world, when the Son of Man will rule gloriously, you who have followed me will also rule, starting with the twelve tribes of Israel. And not only you, but anyone who sacrifices home, family, fields—whatever—because of me will get it all back a hundred times over, not to mention the considerable bonus of eternal life." (THE MESSAGE)

> Jesus replied, "I assure you that when the world is made new and the Son of Man sits upon his glorious throne, you who have been my followers will also sit on twelve thrones, judging the twelve tribes of Israel. And everyone who has given up houses or brothers or sisters or father or mother or children or property, for my sake, will receive a hundred times as much in return and will inherit eternal life." (NLT)

The re-creation of the world. When the world is made new. A promise so breathtaking, so shocking and heartbreakingly beautiful I'm stunned that so many have missed it. Oh yes, we've heard quite a bit about "heaven." But Jesus is clearly not talking about heaven here—he is talking about the re-creation of *all things*, including the earth we love.

If you back up from this point, you can make better sense of the "gospel" of Jesus. First off, the message he proclaimed was the gospel of a coming *kingdom*:

> "The time promised by God has come at last!" he announced. "The Kingdom of God is near! Repent of your sins and believe the Good News!" (Mark 1:14–15 NLT)

> Jesus traveled throughout the region of Galilee, teaching in the synagogues and announcing the Good News about the Kingdom. (Matthew 4:23 NLT)

> Jesus went through all the towns and villages, teaching in their synagogues, proclaiming the good news of the kingdom. (Matthew 9:35)

> "So don't be afraid, little flock. For it gives your Father great happiness to give you the Kingdom." (Luke 12:32 NLT)

> "And this gospel of the kingdom will be preached in the whole world as a testimony to all nations, and then the end will come." (Matthew 24:14)

Jesus announced the coming kingdom of God. He then demonstrated what that promise means—the crippled walk, blind see, deaf hear, the dead are raised to life. His miracles are illustrations for his message, and unforgettable demonstrations they are. No one who saw them could miss the point—the kingdom of God means a Great Restoration. He then announced the renewal of all things right before the Romans seized him, and as if to make sure everyone got the point, he walked out of the grave scot-free three days later—the most dramatic illustration of restoration you could ask for.

We have been looking for the Renewal all our lives. It has been calling to us through every precious memory and every moment of beauty and goodness. It is the promise whispered in every sunrise. Every flower. Every wonderful day of vacation; every pregnancy; the recovery of your health. It calls to us even through our fetishes and fantasies, as C. S. Lewis observed:

> Even in your hobbies, has there not always been some secret attraction which the others are curiously ignorant of—something, not to be identified with, but always on the verge of breaking through, the smell of cut wood in the workshop or the clap-clap of water against the boat's side? Are not all lifelong friendships born at the moment when at last you meet another human being who has some inkling (but faint and uncertain even in the best) of that something which you were born desiring, and which, beneath the flux of other desires and in all the momentary

silences between the louder passions, night and day, year by year, from childhood to old age, you are looking for, watching for, listening for? You have never had it. All the things that have ever deeply possessed your soul have been but hints of it—tantalizing glimpses, promises never quite fulfilled, echoes that died away just as they caught your ear. But if it should really become manifest—if there ever came an echo that did not die away but swelled into the sound itself—you would know it. Beyond all possibility of doubt you would say "Here at last is the thing I was made for."[12]

The thing you are made for is the renewal of all things. God has given you a heart for his kingdom—not the wispy vagaries of a cloudy heaven, but the sharp reality of the world made new. This is one of the most important things you can know about yourself. Did you know this about yourself? When was the last time you told yourself, as you looked in the mirror in the morning, *Good morning; you have a heart for the kingdom.* This explains so much; it will be such an enormous help to you. It explains your anger and all of your addictions. It explains your cry for justice, and it also explains the growing hopelessness, resignation, cynicism, and defeat.

If we will listen with kindness and compassion to our own souls, we will hear the echoes of a hope so precious we can barely put words to it, a wild hope we can hardly bear to embrace. God put it there. He also breathed the corresponding promise into the earth; it is the whisper that keeps coming to us in moments of golden goodness. But of course. "God has made everything beautiful for its own time. He has planted eternity in the human heart" (Ecclesiastes 3:11 NLT). The secret to your unhappiness and the answer to the agony of the earth are one and the same—we are longing for the kingdom of God. We are aching for the restoration of all things.

That is the only hope strong enough, brilliant enough, glorious enough to overcome the heartache of this world.

One morning you will wake, and sunlight will be coming in through the curtains. You will hear the sound of birds singing in the garden; delicious scents of summer will waft in on the breeze. As you open your eyes you will realize how young and whole your body feels. No tormenting thoughts will rush in to assault you; you will realize that your soul feels young and whole too. As you sit up to look around the bedroom filled with light, you will hear the sounds of laughter and running water outside and you will know—it is going to be a wonderful day. Only this hope can serve as the anchor for our souls:

> We who have run for our very lives to God have every reason to grab the promised hope with both hands and never let go. It's an unbreakable spiritual lifeline. (Hebrews 6:19 THE MESSAGE)

So let us chase it now with all of our being.

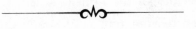

I had a dream about the kingdom of God earlier this year, though at the time I didn't know what was being shown to me.

The setting was nighttime; I was standing on a grassy slope under the stars. It must have been summer because the turf under my feet was lush and thick; the air was warm and sweet. I could see water before me—dark, smooth, glassy water, calm as a lake or tropical bay after sunset. Moonlight was reflecting on the water like you'd expect on a summer night, but so were lanterns, shimmering their warm and happy glow.

Across the water I could hear the sounds of a dinner party not far away. Glasses were clinking, silverware on fine china, but the most alluring of the sounds was the laughter and conversation. It was a lavish yet intimate celebration, filled with joy— like what we long for in the best wedding receptions, or perhaps in a gathering of intimate allies at the estate of a wealthy friend.

The beauty of the scene was quietly enchanting, but what pierced me was the ease of the happiness before me—as if it were the most natural thing in the world, not the fragile happiness we know in our experience.

I was filled with longing when I woke.

CHAPTER 2

The Renewal of All Things

Every man has two
Battles to wage:
In dreams he wrestles with God
Awake, with the sea

ANTONIO MACHADO, *Proverbs and Song Verse*

I t was July when my youngest son and his new wife came
to visit. Stasi and I wanted to take them out for a special
dinner, the kind newlyweds cannot afford themselves. We
booked an evening at the Broadmoor Hotel, a *Forbes* five-
star resort you may have heard of. Picture a gorgeous estate
like you might find in France or Germany—verdant gardens,
flowing fountains, architecture with an "Old World" feel, red
tile roofs, arched turrets, and curving balconies.

We had a lovely evening over a luscious dinner and rich conversation. Olivia, our new daughter-in-law, said, "I've never had an evening like this." Happy, sated, feeling connected with one another, we wandered outside with the sort of leisure you enjoy after a sumptuous meal on a warm summer evening. Stasi was having difficulty walking due to a hip injury, so the two of us chose to rest on a bench while the lovers took a stroll around the lake. The main part of the resort lies across the water, and its lights were shimmering on the dark waters while echoes of laughter and the sounds of dining floated toward us. Closer by, the luscious smells of petunias and summer flowers hanging in baskets surrounded us with nature's perfumes.

Then I remembered my dream.

It had been months since I let the dream slip away, largely because I simply didn't know what to do with it; the happiness and beauty in the dream was nothing near the hard months we were living through. I also didn't know what to make of it at the time, so I'd ventured to ask the Lord what the dream was about. *My Kingdom*, he'd said quietly, reassuringly, with a touch of pride. Yes, it certainly had the "aroma" of the kingdom of God. And yet . . . it did not feel like heaven to me, because the scene was so earthly—water, grass, lanterns, moonlight, a dinner party on a veranda.

Suddenly here we were, not in the dream itself, but in the promise of it. Sitting on the bench with Stasi, I was experiencing a taste of that settled happiness I had seen. Without bidding, my heart whispered, *This is what we were meant for.*

Now the curious thing is this: How did my heart know this? How do *our* hearts know this?

Because Pascal was right—there *was* once a happiness belonging to the human race, and in our hearts we only find now "the faintest traces that remain."[1] Eden was once our home, our long-lost dwelling place, and to Eden we shall return. Thus we keep bumping into the "promise" God placed both in the earth and deep in our hearts, and only by means of the *palingenesia* will we be able to interpret it.

> "People will come from east and west and north and south,
> and will take their places at the feast in the kingdom of
> God." (Luke 13:29)

ALL THINGS NEW

When Jesus used the phrase "at the renewal of all things," he did it casually, almost breezily. You get the impression he assumed his listeners didn't need an explanation or a long defense of the idea. Jesus spoke as though he were simply drawing upon a story and theology his disciples would know quite well. And indeed, these earnest Jews would have immediately found connection with many Old Testament passages stored in their hearts:

> Those the LORD has rescued will return.
> They will enter Zion with singing;

everlasting joy will crown their heads.
Gladness and joy will overtake them,
and sorrow and sighing will flee away. (Isaiah 51:11)

"Then you will look and be radiant,
your heart will throb and swell with joy;
the wealth on the seas will be brought to you,
to you the riches of the nations will come. . . .

"I will make peace your governor
and well-being your ruler.
No longer will violence be heard in your land,
nor ruin or destruction within your borders,
but you will call your walls Salvation
and your gates Praise.
The sun will no more be your light by day,
nor will the brightness of the moon shine on you,
for the Lord will be your everlasting light,
and your God will be your glory.
Your sun will never set again,
and your moon will wane no more;
the Lord will be your everlasting light,
and your days of sorrow will end." (Isaiah 60:5, 17–20)

A contemporary reader just isn't quite sure what to do with such lovely promises as these. The beauty is enough to make my heart ache. But who are they for? When does this take place? We would give our right arm to see a fraction of this happen in our lifetime; half of it would be beyond our wildest dreams. But something in us knows that however much we long for it, we live with the partial here. Moments may come to us, but these passages are referring to something as settled and done as the happiness I saw in my dream. Why has God scattered these promises like wildflowers and precious gems throughout the Scriptures? Is he taunting us?

A few chapters later in Isaiah we find the answer:

> "See, I will create
>> new heavens and a new earth.
> The former things will not be remembered,
>> nor will they come to mind.
> But be glad and rejoice forever
>> in what I will create,
> for I will create Jerusalem to be a delight
>> and its people a joy.
> I will rejoice over Jerusalem
>> and take delight in my people;
> the sound of weeping and of crying
> will be heard in it no more." (65:17–19)

Jesus knew his listeners already embraced this hope; he knew they ached for it and prayed for it. This is the culmination of all the Old Testament promises of a Great Restoration. And of course this passage foreshadows the climax of the book of Revelation, where the entire biblical canon swells to a crescendo like a symphony reaching its glorious finish. Here is the final word of God on his promise to us:

> Then I saw "a new heaven and a new earth," for the first heaven and the first earth had passed away, and there was no longer any sea. I saw the Holy City, the new Jerusalem, coming down out of heaven from God, prepared as a bride beautifully dressed for her husband. And I heard a loud voice from the throne saying, "Look! God's dwelling place is now among the people, and he will dwell with them. They will be his people, and God himself will be with them and be their God. 'He will wipe every tear from their eyes. There will be no more death' or mourning or crying or pain, for the old order of things has passed away."
>
> He who was seated on the throne said, "I am making everything new!" Then he said, "Write this down, for these words are trustworthy and true." (21:1–5)

I know—this is so saturated with meaning, bursting with promise and overflowing with beauty so grand our souls can hardly take it in, like rich dessert. Honestly, it seems too good to be true. We, the survivors of the wreckage of Eden, have grown so accustomed to living on the faintest traces of happiness and restoration, we must slow down and take this proclamation in pieces if we are to understand it, embrace it. This is, after all, the final word of God and the summation of every other biblical text regarding our future. Read it like you would a ransom note if your child had been kidnapped; read it like you would the doctor's report on your cancer—slowly, carefully.

Notice first, that the earth is included, a renewed earth. This passage isn't just about heaven, the Sweet By-and-By. John is shown the New Jerusalem *coming down out of heaven*, an image begun in Revelation 3:12 and repeated a third time in 21:10, just to make sure we get our bearings. The city of God comes to *the earth*. The dwelling of God, which has heretofore been heaven, comes to humans, who dwell on the earth.

Notice also that God promises to make current things new—as opposed to making all new things. If God were wiping away reality as we know it and ushering in a new reality, the phrase would have been "I am making all *new things!*" But that's not what he says, and God is very careful about what he says. Furthermore, if John witnessed some foreign reality being ushered in, he would have reported it so. He's already told us about a meteor named Wormwood, a seven-headed dragon, and some awful beast the Whore of Babylon rides upon. However outrageous, he would have done his best to report the new reality if God had showed him one. But he doesn't; he makes it clear: "I saw Heaven and earth new-created" (21:1 THE MESSAGE).

I find it especially touching that immediately upon saying, "I am making everything new!" our Father God quickly adds, "Write this down, because it is true." Perhaps John the Seer was obviously dumbstruck on this point (wouldn't you be?) and needed to be assured by God, *Yes—this is what I mean.*

Write it down. Perhaps God knew that future readers of such a statement would need the same assurance.

No matter what translation you prefer, the truth of Revelation 21:5 is quite clear:

"Behold, I make all things new." (KJV, NKJV, RSV)

"Behold, I am making all things new." (NASB)

"Look, I am making everything new!" (NLT)

"Look! I'm making everything new." (THE MESSAGE)

The Greek word for "new" is *kainos*—the same word used for the "New" Jerusalem. Certainly we understand that it is not the old Jerusalem coming down out of heaven. It is a freshly remade, renewed Jerusalem. But it is *Jerusalem*—not Baltimore, Baghdad, or Budapest.

REDEMPTION, NOT DESTRUCTION

Many people have the vague but ominous idea that God destroys the current reality and creates a new "heavenly" one. But that is not what Scripture actually says.

For all creation is waiting eagerly for that future day when God will reveal who his children really are. Against its will, all creation was subjected to God's curse. But with eager hope, the creation looks forward to the day when it will join God's children in glorious freedom from death and decay. For we know that all creation has been groaning as in the pains of childbirth right up to the present time. And we believers also groan, even though we have the Holy Spirit within us as a foretaste of future glory, for we long for our bodies to be released from sin and suffering. We, too, wait with eager hope for the day when God will give us our full rights as his adopted children, including the new bodies he has promised us. (Romans 8:19–23 NLT)

Paul teaches us that creation—meaning the earth and the animal kingdom—longs for the day of *its* redemption, when "it will join God's children in glorious freedom from death and decay" (v. 21). Clearly that does not imply destruction; far from it. Paul anticipated a joyful day when creation shares in the eternity of the children of God:

The created world itself can hardly wait for what's coming next. Everything in creation is being more or less held back. God reins it in until both creation and all the creatures are ready and can be released at the same moment into the glorious times ahead. (Romans 8:19–21 THE MESSAGE)

The glorious times ahead, when all things are made new. Now, yes—there are some ominous passages about the end of this age. Peter gives us one of the definitive texts:

———

Long ago by God's word the heavens came into being and the earth was formed out of water and by water. By these waters also the world of that time was deluged and destroyed. By the same word the present heavens and earth are reserved for fire, being kept for the day of judgment and destruction of the ungodly. . . . The day of the Lord will come like a thief. The heavens will disappear with a roar; the elements will be destroyed by fire, and the earth and everything done in it will be laid bare. (2 Peter 3:5–7, 10)

Fiery words, to be sure, filled with images on par with the best of Hollywood's "end of the world" movies. But let's examine this carefully. First off, Peter points to the Flood of Noah's day as the image for the end of the age: "By these waters also the world of that time was deluged and destroyed" (v. 6). Therefore, we can be confident he does not mean *annihilated*, vaporized like the Death Star, for the very obvious reason that the earth was *not* destroyed by the Flood—it is still right here where it's always been. You've been living on it all your life. The Flood *cleansed* the earth, renewed it. Noah and his family stepped out of the ark onto a restored earth, to begin again.

Peter then turns from water to fire as the element by which the earth we love is scoured. Fire is also used for cleansing throughout the Scriptures; you recall that Paul said our life's work will be tested in the fire, like gold. The good remains; only the dross is burned away (1 Corinthians 3:13–15).

Remember now—it was Peter who asked Jesus the question back in Matthew 19 that our Lord responded to by announcing the "renewal of all things." Peter was right there; he heard his Master say it. And so he concludes his passage on the end of the age with these words:

> But in keeping with his promise we are looking forward to a new heaven and a new earth, where righteousness dwells. (2 Peter 3:13)

For too long Christians have misunderstood their destiny. We have thought we would leave the earth we love and go up to an ethereal "heaven" somewhere. Not so. Dallas Willard was one of the most brilliant and influential Christian leaders and thinkers of the twentieth century. He spent a great deal of effort helping his readers understand the gospel of Jesus, which centers around this very truth:

> The life we now have as the persons we now are will continue, and continue in the universe in which we now exist. Our experience will be much clearer, richer, and deeper, of course . . . rooted in the broader and more fundamental reality of God's kingdom and will accordingly have far greater scope and power.[2]

The "you" that you are and the world we inhabit will *continue.* Scholar and theologian N. T. Wright has written a great deal on this matter; he assures us that the early Christians "believed that God was going to do for the whole cosmos what he had done for Jesus at Easter."[3] Peter picked up the theme of the *palingenesia* in Acts, declaring the Renewal the Jews had long anticipated, only now made clear and possible through Jesus Christ. In one of his famous sermons he declared exactly what his Lord taught him:

> "Repent, then, and turn to God, so that your sins may be wiped out, that times of refreshing may come from the Lord, and that he may send the Messiah, who has been appointed for you—even Jesus. Heaven must receive him until the time comes for God to restore everything, as he promised long ago through his holy prophets." (Acts 3:19–21)

Jesus is in heaven *until* the promised Day when God will "restore everything," or "until the time for the final restoration of all things" (NLT). The Greek word used here for "restore" is another stunning word: *apokatastasis*, which in both biblical and secular usage meant to put something back in its original condition. The verb form is used in Mark 3:1–6 when Jesus heals a man's withered hand (demonstrating restoration). Peter is both reaffirming and elaborating upon a long-held Jewish conviction that the Messiah will return things "to their original state, the universal renewal of the world which reestablishes the original integrity of creation."[4] Thus, Wright argues that "it is not we who go to heaven, it is heaven that comes to earth . . . the final answer to the Lord's prayer, that God's kingdom will come and his will be done on earth as it is in heaven."[5]

Breathtaking. How is it I have missed this all my life? And I know I'm not alone.

Nirvana, "total nonexistence" as the Buddhist hopes, or "everlasting tranquility of death" as Hindus expect, is as unimpressive as the false Christian belief in the total destruction of creation.[6] Annihilation is not nearly as impressive as *redemption*.

When we begin to unpack the teaching of Jesus and his disciples in light of the Jewish expectation—dramatically illustrated by miracles performed by Jesus like giving the blind their sight and raising the dead—the light of the Great Renewal begins to break through the darkness in which we have long dwelt. God does not merely scrap creation and our intended roles along with it. He restores everything.

I know, I know—it's a lot to take in. This is a total reframing for most of us, even though it has been right there in the Scriptures for centuries. Take a moment; take a deep breath. Get a glass of water if you need to, or something stronger. You've just been told your future is "the restoration of all things," real things, the restoration of everything *you* love.

No wonder it begins with a glorious feast of celebration! "Blessed are those who are invited to the wedding supper of the Lamb!" (Revelation 19:9). This wedding reception is also foreshadowed in the Jewish expectation of the coming kingdom:

———

> On this mountain the LORD Almighty will prepare
> > a feast of rich food for all peoples,
> a banquet of aged wine—
> > the best of meats and the finest of wines.
> On this mountain he will destroy
> > the shroud that enfolds all peoples,
> the sheet that covers all nations;
> > he will swallow up death forever.
> The Sovereign LORD will wipe away the tears
> > from all faces;
> he will remove his people's disgrace
> from all the earth. (Isaiah 25:6–8)

Perhaps this was what I saw in my dream.

There is a wonderful, tangible depiction of this feast in the book and film *The Fellowship of the Ring*. Bilbo Baggins is celebrating his 111th birthday with an extravagant celebration he throws at his own generous expense. It takes place on a late-summer evening; the countryside is in full bloom. Lanterns are hanging in the trees. Fireworks are going off over an outdoor party—picnic tables, a dance floor, pavilion, live music, laughter, celebration. An entire community is having the time of their lives. When our eldest son, Sam, was getting married and planning the reception, he said, "I want Bilbo's party." Don't you? The joy, ease, companionship, the lightheartedness of it; there is no clock ticking, no curfew, nobody's going to call the police—it just gets to go on and on.

Jesus is personally looking forward to this celebration immensely: "Truly I tell you, I will not drink again from the fruit of the vine until that day when I drink it new in the kingdom of God" (Mark 14:25). Jesus assumes a day is coming when very real things like drinking wine together will take place in the kingdom of God. When all things are made new.

We have many chapters before us to unpack what the renewal of all things will mean for us, and some unpacking it needs. What about heaven? What is included in "all things"? Does everyone participate? Are we getting close to its arrival? Our imaginations are impoverished and need a good bit of resuscitation. But for now, let us pause and allow this to begin to seep into our being: God promises the renewal of all things. He promises to make all things new.

WHAT DOES RESTORATION LOOK LIKE?

Jesus Christ is the forerunner for the Great Renewal, "the beginning and the firstborn from among the dead" (Colossians 1:18). He died, as everyone has and will. But on the third day he was raised to life, leaving his grave clothes folded neatly in the tomb. (A very touching detail, I might add, as if to say, "And that's that," like a man putting away his flannel pajamas now that winter is past.) On Easter morning Jesus walked out of the grave radiantly alive, restored, and everyone recognized him. The "new" Jesus is not someone or something else now; he is the Jesus they loved and knew. He walked with them, had meals with them—just like before. The most striking thing about the post-resurrection activities of Jesus is that they were so remarkably *ordinary*:

> Early in the morning, Jesus stood on the shore, but the disciples did not realize that it was Jesus.
>
> He called out to them, "Friends, haven't you any fish?"
>
> "No," they answered.
>
> He said, "Throw your net on the right side of the boat and you will find some." When they did, they were unable to haul the net in because of the large number of fish. . . .
>
> When they landed, they saw a fire of burning coals there with fish on it, and some bread.
>
> Jesus said to them, "Bring some of the fish you have just caught." So Simon Peter climbed back into the boat and dragged the net ashore. It was full of large fish, 153, but even with so many the net was not torn. Jesus said to them, "Come and have breakfast." None of the disciples dared ask him, "Who are you?" They knew it was the Lord. Jesus came, took the bread and gave it to them, and did the same with the fish. (John 21:4–6, 9–13)

This is such a homely scene, so commonplace, the sort of thing you'd expect to run into along the shore of Lake Michigan or the Mississippi. Just a group of guys hanging out at the beach, cooking breakfast for some friends. Jesus' restored life is surprisingly like his "former" life. As will be drinking wine at the feast; as will be the feast itself (how many of you realize you *eat* in the life to come?!). The Great Renewal rescues us from all the vague, ethereal, unimaginable visions we've been given of an eternal life Somewhere Up Above. When Jesus speaks of the Restoration, he does so in very tangible terms, pointing to the recovery of normal things like houses and lands:

> "Truly I tell you, at the renewal of all things, when the Son of Man sits on his glorious throne . . . everyone who has left houses or brothers or sisters or father or mother or wife or children or fields for my sake will receive a hundred times as much and will inherit eternal life." (Matthew 19:28–29)

There is no bait and switch here. The renewal of all things simply means that the earth you love—all your special places and treasured memories—is restored and renewed and given back to you. Forever. Nobody seems to have heard this or paid much attention to it because, for one thing, nobody I know is fantasizing about it. When was the last time you eavesdropped on a conversation at Starbucks about the restoration of all things? And for another thing, everybody I talk to still has these anemic, wispy views of heaven, as a place up there somewhere, where we go to attend the eternal-worship-service-in-the-sky.

Meanwhile we fantasize about that boat we'd love to get or the trip to Italy, the chocolate éclair or the girl in the cubicle next door. Of course we do—we are made for utter happiness.

But the restoration of all things—now that would change everything.

ALL CREATION IS PROCLAIMING

God has been declaring the promise of the Great Renewal faithfully, repeatedly, through nature since the dawn of time. How have we missed it? Creation is no accident; it is a *proclamation*. A wild, bold declaration. (This will rescue you from so many things; pay very close attention.) Every spring and summer God plays out for us the day of the Great Restoration with wild, splashy boldness. It meant more to me this year than ever before.

The-year-I-wish-to-never-live-again also included nine months of chronic pain for Stasi, which ended in a total hip replacement (a brutal surgery I won't describe here). Following the surgery I spent two very long days in the hospital at her side. Hospitals are melancholy places. Don't get me wrong—they can also be places of immense relief and hope. I think the people who serve there have taken a heroic stand on the side of hope. But let's be honest—on the user side, no one is there because they *want* to be, unless they are there to have a baby; they are there because something is wrong, often very wrong. People don't play pickup games of Frisbee in the halls of hospitals; you don't hear folks loudly cracking jokes. The corridors are filled with hushed tones and a shared sobriety. Apart from the maternity floor, the staff, patients, and concerned visitors all agree: *This is serious business. Somebody could be dying in that room you just walked by.*

After what felt like a week in a hospital room with my dear love, I slipped into that mental space where you think this is all there is in the world—monitors going off all day long, staff coming in and out with urgency, the stupor of drug-induced rest, the IV and cold rooms and artificial everything. I left her room at five thirty to go grab us some dinner, and as I stepped outside I was washed over by a wave of summer evening. It was wonderfully warm; my body relaxed immediately. My eyes blinked to take in the colors. I saw cumulus clouds building towers for their evening show. Meadowlarks across the field were singing and singing. The aspens were shimmering in a gentle breeze; the rich scents of summer flowers enveloped me. I was suddenly immersed in all the wonderful fragrances and feelings of *life* in its summer lushness.

It was like experiencing the *palingenesia.*

Summer is God's annual pageant on behalf of the restoration of all things, all nature practically shouting at us because we are tone deaf. That's why we love it so much. We pack up the car and head to the lake or the park; we break out the grill and have friends over, laughing late into the starlit evening; we dive into waters and bake in the sun, and in this way we get a good, deep drink of Restoration. It's no coincidence the classic surfing road-trip film is entitled *The Endless Summer.* I'm telling you, the message is *everywhere.*

———

God is trying to do two things with the promise in the earth and in our hearts: he is trying to woo us into hopeful expectation, and he is attempting to lift our gaze to the horizon so we might live for the real thing that is coming.

To be sure, it feels wintry enough still: but often in the very early spring it feels like that . . . the spring comes down slowly down this way; but the great thing is that the corner has been turned. There is, of course, this difference, that in the natural spring the crocus cannot choose whether it will respond or not. We can. We have the power either of withstanding the spring, and sinking back into the cosmic winter, or of going on into these "high midsummer pomps" in which our leader, the Son of Man, already dwells, and to which he is calling us. It remains with us to follow or not, to die in this winter, or to go on into that spring and that summer.[7]

We have quite a stunning present to unpack, dear readers, and chapters to do it some justice. But we must prepare our hearts to receive such a gift, or it will wash over us like rain on hard ground.

I went into the woods the other day with a box of shells and an old Remington 870 pump-action shotgun. As I left the house I told Stasi, "You will hear some shots, and probably some shouting. Don't worry; I am okay."

As soon as I got into the forest I began blasting away at rotting tree stumps. When the shells were all gone, I put down the gun and took to bashing the dead branches of fallen limbs against the trunks of trees, exploding them, over and over and over. And shouting; there was lots of shouting.

I was in the anger stage of grief, and I needed to get it out.

CHAPTER 3

Let Us Be Honest

*Our imagination so powerfully magnifies
time, by continual reflections upon it, and so
diminishes eternity . . . for want of reflection, that
we make a nothing of eternity and an eternity
of nothing. . . . This is a dangerous game.*

BLAISE PASCAL, *Pensées*

Stasi and I raised three sons, three very boy-ish boys—every-puddle-must-be-jumped-in, every-tree-climbed boys. If Tom Sawyer or the Lost Boys from *Peter Pan* had grown up in a real family, they might have been at our house. Our home was filled with the whoops of an American Indian war dance or the fierce sounds of light sabers as young Jedi fought for the galaxy. Come bedtime we had a ritual for years and years where I would lie on the floor of their shared room and tell them stories about the Wild West. Those tales always began, "Once upon a time there were three cowboys named Sam, Blaine, and Luke . . ."

Our boys had something very rare in this world—they had a childhood.

I can still remember the feeling in the pit of my stomach the night before Sam left for college. Our little clan had gathered in the family room to pray, each of us knowing some sort of ending was upon us, each of us not wanting to name it. We sat in a circle on the floor—the floor that had held so many Christmas mornings and wrestling matches, the floor where we welcomed our first dog as a puppy and also said good-bye to him in old age. I was trying to find something to say; the words of Bob Cratchit kept coming to mind, at the loss of Tiny Tim: "But however and whenever we part from one another, I am sure we shall none of us forget . . . this first parting that there was among us."[1] I tried to mumble a few words about, "We love you, Sam . . ."

Luke simply threw himself on his oldest brother's lap, acting out what everyone felt.

I hate good-byes. I really do.

Blaine would remain behind two more years; he and Luke were thick as thieves during that season. Then came Blaine's turn to head off to college out of state. Luke was only a year into his high school sojourn, and I knew it would prove very hard and lonely; my father's heart ached for him. So every morning I would wake before Luke and make us both a cup of tea (he loved tea). We'd share those early-morning moments in the kitchen, sipping tea, sometimes talking, sometimes just being quiet. Then we would pray together, and I would send Luke into his day. This was our ritual every morning for three years—tea and prayers.

As May of his senior year approached, I could feel a yawning pit opening in my stomach again, this time even bigger. I knew the morning was coming when we would have our last cup of tea. High school would end, summer would pass too quickly, and Luke would head off to college himself. These days would be over, forever. When Stasi and I returned home after dropping him off at the university he had chosen, we walked into an empty house. I went downstairs into Luke's room, turned off the lights, and shut the door. An era had ended. Twenty-four years of life with sons at home, and in one moment the golden days of boyhood and family were gone.

The next morning I made just one cup of tea.

Like our shadow, the truth is always there; we don't often look at it, but we know—life is a long series of good-byes. You've already said good-bye to your childhood years, and with them probably your hometown and the house you were raised in, not to mention your childhood friends. The best of us might hang on to one or two playmates from our youth, but catching pollywogs with Danny down in the creek just isn't recovered through a Christmas card. If you had a beloved childhood pet, you have said that hard good-bye as well; I've had clients for whom it remained one of their life's greatest wounds. Most of us said farewell to first sweethearts, feeling as though some golden part of our innocence was left behind with them. Most of you have left your first apartment after being married and all the sweet memories there.

If you stop and think about it, you've said a lot of good-byes in your life so far. And fight it as we may, we know down deep that many more are coming. I think that's why I hate even small good-byes, like when the kids leave after a Thanksgiving visit. Stasi said to me last time, "This is our life now—saying good-bye."

Oh, friends—this is why hope is so very precious. It is our lifeline, the anchor of our souls. And this is why it is so important to know where our hope is, to help it land in the right places.

PROTECTING HOPE

I always felt it strange that God needed to command us to love him. (It is the first and greatest of all the commandments.) Now I see better. When God calls us to love him as our "first love," it is not only because he deserves to hold that place in our hearts, but also because he knows what pain will come when we get that out of order. If you give the part of your soul that is meant for God to lesser things, they will break your heart because they cannot possibly come through for you in the ways God can. Only he will never leave you or forsake you. The command is a rescue from disaster.

Many of you have begun to discover the joy and freedom loving God brings to the rest of your life. Keeping God as our first love, we are not destroyed when others fail to love us well; we are able to weather criticism, loneliness, and rejection. Our other loves are able to find their whole and wholesome expression, and we are able to flourish as human beings. Anchored in True Love, our hearts can go on to love. Because we have first things first, as the saying goes.

Hope functions in the same way.

When our hopes are in their proper places, attached to the right things, not only do we flourish better as human beings, but we are rescued from a thousand heartbreaks. For not all hopes are created equal; there are casual hopes, precious hopes, and ultimate hopes.

Casual hopes are the daily variety: "I sure hope it doesn't rain this weekend"; "I hope we can get tickets to the game"; "I really hope this flight is on time." Nothing wrong with this brand of hope; it is human nature to have it. I think it is the sign of a healthy soul when we often use the words "*I hope.*" My wife does. "I hope this pie turns out," meaning she cares about the dinner she is hosting. "I hope we get to the Tetons next year," meaning she cares about dreams and family memories. Hope shows your heart is still alive.

But of course, those casual hopes are nothing when compared to our precious hopes: "I hope this pregnancy goes well"; "I hope God hears my prayers for Sally"; "I hope the CT scan turns out to reveal nothing at all." Precious hopes are far deeper to our hearts, and they tend to fuel our most earnest prayers.

Deeper still lie our ultimate hopes, our life-and-death

hopes. I would suggest that the only things that belong in the category of ultimate hopes are the things that will destroy your heart and soul if they are not fulfilled. "I hope God can forgive me." "I hope somehow my mistakes can be redeemed." "I hope I will see you again."

You'll notice that many people have let their hopes go wandering—they have made casual hopes into precious hopes and turned genuinely precious hopes into critical or ultimate hopes. The person who commits suicide because their loved one chose another has taken a precious hope and made it the outcome of their very being.

I would say that when a casual hope is deferred, we are disappointed but no more. We are downcast for a moment or a day. When a precious hope is dashed, it can really break your heart. You may not recover for a week or five years, depending on the loss and the other resources of your life. "Hope deferred makes the heart sick" (Proverbs 13:12). Doesn't it, though?

But when an *ultimate* hope goes unanswered, the result is devastation from which you will never recover.

Maybe another barometer would look like this: When our casual hopes are suddenly in question, they elicit worry, but nothing more. Precious hopes in question can usher in fear and anxiety. Ultimate hopes that suddenly seem uncertain shake the soul to its core. And I will be forthright with you—very few things deserve the place in your heart made for ultimate hope.

Here is my point: the renewal of all things is meant to be your first hope in the way that God is your First Love. If it isn't the answer to your wildest dreams, if you aren't ready at this very moment to sell everything and buy this field, then you have placed your hopes somewhere else.

Nearly everyone has.

We cannot move forward in our search for the *palingenesia* until we face the truth honestly. Otherwise, this will just be a curiosity; interesting, but not the rescue our hearts so desperately need. We fight this hope. We hear about the Renewal and think to ourselves, *Well, isn't that nice; I'd never heard it put that way*, and go right on with our desperate search for the kingdom now.

You have a heart for the kingdom, for the Great Restoration. I said it might be the most important thing to know about yourself; it is a lens by which you can understand your longings, fears, addictions, anger—not to mention the actions of the human race. Where is your kingdom heart these days? Are you embarrassed by it? What are you presently doing with it? What are you fantasizing about? Where we take our fantasies is a helpful way to know what we are doing with our kingdom heart.

LOOKING FOR THE KINGDOM

The north shore of Kauai is one of the most beautiful places on earth, and the pastures above the cliffs overlooking Anini Beach are some of the last open lands in that paradise. From those verdant meadows you can look out on the whales and dolphins playing in the Pacific, watch the breakers roll in and crash over the reef below. It is an enchanting place that casts an Eden-like spell on even the most cynical tourist. A friend of ours has been advocating for the protection of those gorgeous meadows; he took us there last winter to see a view that may soon be available only to the very rich. The pastures have already been marked out for small five-acre "ranchettes," each plot going for several million; add to that the home required by the development and the bill will run more than $20 million. "The young rich have discovered Kauai," our friend told us. "Zuckerberg has a home here; so do the guys from Apple and Google. This is the place to be."

We stood there watching the gulls and frigate birds soaring on the warm updrafts, drinking in the beauty only money can apparently buy. It had been raining; a rainbow appeared over the lush cliffs to our right. The untouched beauty of the place feels like it has been held in time since the islands were formed; unblemished beauty. Forgetting what the promise means, my heart began to ache again for life as it was meant to be, and I started to scramble internally trying to figure out how we could grab our own little slice of Eden.

"They are looking for the kingdom," Stasi said. "They are trying to buy the kingdom."

And with that, the spell was broken. Suddenly the emptiness of it all became clear—not the longing for heaven on earth, but the grasping to buy it, to arrange for our piece of it apart from the *palingenesia*.

Now, most of the human race doesn't have the kind of money that allows them to purchase paradise—we sure don't—but that doesn't stop our ravenous hunger or desperate searching. I was sitting in the waiting room of my dentist yesterday, catching up on some light reading. The magazine I happened to choose was devoted to mountain biking. The article I opened to was entitled "Kingdom Come," a location piece about the glorious biking available in rural Vermont. As if heaven had come to earth. But every sport has its fantasy periodical, its pornography—surfing, skiing, sailing, travel, you name it. Those luscious photo journals filled with gorgeous places where Shangri-la can be found.

Nathaniel Hawthorne wrote, "Our creator would never have made such lovely days and given us the deep hearts to enjoy them above and beyond all thought unless we were meant to be immortal."[2] The longing isn't the issue; our timing is. We keep mistaking the message of the promise and forget—we must wait for the renewal of all things if we would truly find heaven on earth.

I am troubled by the growing sophistication of video games and virtual reality. The technology has jumped light-years since Pac-Man and Mario Brothers. Now we have complex story lines set in breathtaking fantasy worlds; there you get to have marvelous adventures and do heroic deeds. The Assassin's Creed series has sold close to a hundred million copies as of June 2015, the Elder Scrolls franchise more than forty million copies worldwide.[3] The reason for their wild popularity goes far beyond escapism; the "kingdoms" found in those games touch the very hunger in our souls God made for the *palingenesia*.

———

But perhaps you are not a gamer, so let me point you to something far more common: the "bucket list." The euphemism is household vernacular, at least in the Western world where incomes provide some room for daydreaming. "What's on your bucket list?" is standard cocktail party fare and a question used in interviews when the potential employer is trying to "get to know you."

I've had an embarrassing reaction to bucket lists for some time, and only recently have I understood why. Friends and acquaintances will speak excitedly about something on their bucket list—sailing to Tahiti, visiting the Holy Land, taking a motorcycle trek through Asia—and I feel completely baffled. At first I thought it was because I don't have a bucket list, can't even name the top things that would make my list, and I thought, *Maybe I don't allow myself to dream.* But clarity came as I thought more about the Restoration.

The renewal of all things is meant to be the center of our view of the world, our hopes, and our tangible expectations as we plan our lives going forward. The phrase *bucket list* comes from the expression "kick the bucket," the day we give it all up. A bucket list means those things we hope to do before we die. Meaning, it's now or never, baby. Bucket list mentality is very revealing and even more tragic, because it betrays our belief that this life *really* is our only chance. After all—we think the earth is destroyed and we go to the pews in the sky. No wonder the human race grows more desperate in our search for kingdom counterfeits.

I believe this is the secret behind the explosion of sexual

deviancy across the planet. When *millions* of children are traf-ficked annually into the sex trade, when pornography and prostitution are billion-dollar industries, when one in four girls and one in six boys will be sexually abused before they reach adulthood, you have a world where sexual desire has gone psychopathic.[4] Next step is the virtual reality I named above; when intimate erotic experience far beyond normal human relations becomes available in any fashion, anytime, we will lose millions more souls to the dark addiction.

As I explained in chapter 1, human beings are ravenous creatures. Our hope is ungrounded, untethered. A famished craving compels us toward some sort of relief. The traditional institutions meant to anchor human psychology have all but crumbled, releasing the ravenous beast to range unchecked into any and every dark option. Inevitably, something or someone gets in the way, and we are ready to kill. Thus the hatred that is exploding around the world. We live in wicked, violent times; I fear worse may happen by the time this book is published.

The hatred speaks of a *desperation*. The desperation speaks of our soul's unbelief in the Restoration. It's that simple.

FACING THE INEVITABLE

A friend of mine, a gifted playwright, won an award for his script about a man dying of AIDS. The protagonist is an endearing young artist who grows weaker and more frail through the course of the play. Even so, he has a touching

compulsion to take Polaroid shots of everyone and everything he cares about, looking at the images as they appear and
tucking them away in his satchel. It is a poignant obsession,
of course, because he is dying, and no attempt to hang on to
his world will prevent that. We the audience experience a sad
empathy for him: *Poor fellow—he won't be needing those.* And
miss the point entirely. We are he.

You will say the last good-bye to your parents. It is
inevitable.

God forbid you have to say the last good-bye to your
child.

What is it, my readers, that you hope to hang on to? If
you love your athletic condition, surely you realize it cannot go on forever; eventually your body will succumb to age
and your performance will diminish every year. Inexorably.
If you relish your mind, you understand that your mind will
dim with age; even if you dodge the great leveler dementia,
you will forget many things, and may eventually have the
mental capacity of a small child. And the people you love?
You will lose them or they you; your very life is but a passing
breeze, "each of us is but a breath" (Psalm 39:5 NLT). The
fall and winter of your life will come; they are perhaps upon
many of you even now. There is no holding back that winter.

You understand, dear friends, that you will say good-bye
to everyone you love and everything you hold dear.

I am not a fatalist, not even a pessimist. I find joy in many
things. I am practically a hedonist in my love for life. A novel
based on the life of Vincent van Gogh bears a title I used

———

to swear by: *Lust for Life*. But if we are going to embrace the hope God is so lavishly extending us, we must be honest about the nature of *this* life. As Henri Nouwen admitted,

> Our life is a short time in expectation, a time in which sadness and joy kiss each other at every moment. There is a quality of sadness that pervades all the moments of our lives. It seems that there is no such thing as a clear-cut pure joy, but that even in the most happy moments of our existence we sense a tinge of sadness. In every satisfaction, there is an awareness of limitations. In every success, there is the fear of jealousy. Behind every smile, there is a tear. In every embrace, there is loneliness. In every friendship, distance. And in all forms of light, there is the knowledge of surrounding darkness.[5]

Or as Paul said, "And if our hope in Christ is only for this life, we are more to be pitied than anyone in the world" (1 Corinthians 15:19 NLT).

The first time I lost a dear, dear friend was in May of 1998. Brent and I had just coauthored our first book; we shared a counseling practice. He was killed in a climbing accident on the first retreat we led together. I remember the grief well; it was excruciating. I remember saying I wouldn't wish it on my worst enemy. Death is such a violent assault on God's design for our lives, our souls experience it as trauma. It took me years to recover.

And then this summer it happened again. I know exactly

where I was when the phone call came; I can describe to you the gravel driveway and the bushes in front of me, the wood-pile beneath them. Trauma does that—it sears memories into your soul like a branding iron.

Craig and I met in 1979. We shared a love of backpacking and wild beauty. We both had come out of the drug culture and into the Jesus movement. We had worked as janitors at the same church. Over the years we watched each other start our families, move to new jobs. Seven years ago he was diagnosed with leukemia. He went through a number of research trials; some of them took him to hell and back. But this spring there were promising signs—the new protocol seemed to be working marvelously. His doctors said he was a month or two away from remission. Suddenly he began to have abdominal pains; it struck in May, as it had with Brent, a timing that carried the same sort of extra stab as my father dying on Father's Day weekend. Craig and his wife, Lori, had to miss Luke's wedding to get down to Houston for more tests.

A CT scan revealed the worst of all nightmares—his cancer had morphed into lymphoma. Some of you have lost a loved one to lymphoma, and you know what that diagnosis means. It is a voracious and untreatable cancer; it is the kind of diagnosis where they simply tell you, "Get your affairs in order."

The thing about grief is, it opens the door to the room in your soul where all your other grief is stored. Which can be a good thing if you handle it well, take the opportunity to heal the neglected grief. But still. Life begins to feel like it is only and always going to be loss. After I threw my phone across the neighbor's yard, I took a very long walk. Then Stasi, Sam, Susie, and I sat on the porch for an hour or so. We cried, but said very little. What is to be said? Finally, Sam spoke:

"There is only Jesus."

Sam is a keen observer of people and situations; he has a quick eye for the truth no one else wants to admit. He is the boy in the fable who points out that the emperor is buck naked. It was only two months since he had buried his first child, Patrick. Now it would be Craig. He knew what this meant for me. For all of us. But I think he had also traveled pretty quickly to the inevitable—that one day *he* will be getting that phone call, carrying the news about his mom or me.

"Yes," I said. "There is only Jesus. What you believe about the kingdom changes everything."

Odd things come to your mind at times like these. I thought of that passage from Ecclesiastes, claiming, "It is better to go to a house of mourning than to go to a house of feasting" (7:2a). I've always hated that verse. I've been to houses of mourning; those were the hardest visits I have made in my life. When Brent was killed, I was the one to bring the news to his wife and two boys. I will never forget the wailing of those boys. Now I would have to make another of those visits; not just a visit, but to linger there. I was thinking about writing this book as we sat on the porch, and the kindness of God in having me deep in these very truths at a time of massive loss, recurring loss. Solomon was simply trying to say that until we face the facts, we are deluded human beings, "for death is the destiny of everyone; the living should take this to heart" (v. 2b).

There is only the kingdom, friends. Everything else will slip through your fingers, no matter how strong your grasp. Why do we fight this hope, keeping it at arm's length? We nod in appreciation but ask it to stay outside our yard. It is as though some power or force is colluding with our deepest fears and keeping us all under a spell. Pascal understood:

Nothing is so important to man as his own state, nothing is so formidable to him as eternity; and thus it is not natural that there should be men indifferent to the loss of their existence, and to the perils of everlasting suffering. They are quite different with regard to all other things. They are afraid of mere trifles; they foresee them; they feel them. And this same man who spends so many days and nights in rage and despair for the loss of office, or for some imaginary insult to his honour, is the very one who knows without anxiety and without emotion that he will lose all by death. It is a monstrous thing to see in the same heart and at the same time this sensibility to trifles and this strange insensibility to the greatest objects. It is an incomprehensible enchantment, and a supernatural slumber, which indicates as its cause an all-powerful force.[6]

Pascal was bewildered, dumbfounded. What is this dark enchantment that keeps the human race from facing the inevitable? You cannot protect your hope until you face the inevitable; maturity means living without denial. But we are mainlining denial; we are shooting it straight into our veins. We are grasping at every possible means to avoid the inevitable. We give our hopes to all sorts of kingdom counterfeits and substitutes; we give our hearts over to mere morsels. We mistake the promise of the kingdom for the reality and give our being over to its shadow.

But when you raise the white flag, when you finally accept the truth that you will lose everything one way or another, utterly, irrevocably—then the Restoration is news beyond your wildest dreams.

WHAT IF?

Let me take you back now to the last cup of tea, Luke's parting, and the ending of our family's childhood era. It was the Saturday of his high school graduation. We had been through two others before and knew the ritual well. I believe in rituals; they are the last signposts left in a culture of impermanence. But as we sat in the bleachers, unable to stop the unfolding ceremony, watching Luke slowly approach the stage in cap and gown, I was on the brink of sobbing shamelessly. *How is this not just loss?* my heart cried to God. *Tell me—how is everything not just loss?* At that moment everything felt like loss.

Jesus replied immediately, *Oh, John—nothing is lost.*

Some of you may have experienced in a sermon or during personal Bible study, perhaps in a time of prayer or in a counselor's office, the ability of Jesus to communicate an entire concept in a single moment. You have a revelation. The Creator of our mind and soul can give to us a sweeping understanding as if by transfusion. If I put into words the revelation given in that moment in the forty-second row at an ordinary high school commencement, Jesus showed me something like this:

> When the kingdom comes, my dear, heartbroken friend, nothing that was precious to you in this life will be lost. No memory, no event, none of your story or theirs, nothing is lost. How could it be lost? It is all held safe in the heart of the infinite God, who encompasses all things. Held safe outside of time in the treasuries of the kingdom, which transcends yet honors all time. This will all be given back to you at the Restoration, just as surely as your sons will come back to you. Nothing is lost.

The effect was nearly instantaneous. I went from a desolate parent saying good-bye—not just to our last child but to an entire era—to a beloved son who had just been given a sneak preview of the Christmas morning that will come upon all the earth. I underwent a complete emotional transformation. All time had stopped in the moment before that moment; now I was completely fine. My body relaxed back into the chair like a man who had just set forth on a Caribbean cruise. I wanted to shout out, "You can carry on—I'm good now."

Nothing is lost.

If you will just let go of your anger and cynicism for a moment, just allow it to be true for a moment, well then—your heart is going to take a pretty deep breath.

I dreamed of the kingdom again last night.

This time I saw horses, fifty or sixty at least, galloping through fields of tall grasses. The grace and freedom of their thundering stride was captivating. Behind them rose mountains, majestic, rugged, and snowcapped; it looked like the Patagonian steppe. But there was a freshness, a crispness to the scene, like the morning of creation.

I thought perhaps they were wild horses; then I saw riders among them.

Suddenly I, too, was among them, riding with them. We came to an embankment and stream crossing. Horse and rider amended their gait, and soon as we were over, took off again like the wind. It was a glorious game of sorts, a romp.

When I woke I thought, Surely I am making this up. I had breakfast and drove to work. There, on a city corner, where I have never seen such a sight in twenty years of living here, were riders on horseback. As if Jesus were saying, Now do you believe me?

Yes. I do.

CHAPTER 4

The New Earth

*He thought his happiness was complete when, as
he meandered aimlessly along, suddenly he stood by
the edge of a full-fed river. Never in his life had he
seen a river before—this sleek, sinuous, full-bodied
animal, chasing and chuckling, gripping things with
a gurgle and leaving them with a laugh, to fling itself
on fresh playmates that shook themselves free. . . .
All was a-shake and a-shiver—glints and gleams
and sparkles, rustle and swirl, chatter and bubble.
The Mole was bewitched, entranced, fascinated.*

KENNETH GRAHAME, *The Wind in the Willows*

I think I remember every tent I ever slept in. My father
owned an old WWII army surplus model; we would take
it on fishing trips into the Kern River. The musty smell of
oiled canvas still means high adventure to me, fifty years

later. I still have the first backpacking tent I bought myself in 1979; it leaks too much to use, but I can't bear to let it go, with all those memories it carries for me. Right up through this summer, when I took a solo trip into the mountains to remember backpacking with Craig, I love waking up in a tent. It reaches back to that magical sense of adventure that comes so naturally to a boy, when I would wake in my little tepee and realize that a day of endless adventures was waiting right outside my door.

There is nothing like stepping out your door into a bright and beckoning world. This is why people vacation in beautiful places. It is also the secret to the stories you love—that magical moment when the hero or heroine steps into a brave new world. You might still remember that lovely catch of breath and skip of heartbeat the first time you followed Lucy through the back of the wardrobe into a snowy wood. Older readers may recall a scene from the first Star Wars film, when young Luke Skywalker steps out of his home in the deserts of Tatooine to watch not one but *two* suns setting into the horizon. Two suns brilliantly evoked in a moment that sense of "otherness" and wonder. Personally, I love the moment in *The Alchemist* when Santiago embarks with the caravan across the Sahara.

We are preparing our hearts to receive the hope that alone can be the anchor of our souls. One day soon you will step into a renewed earth, a young earth, sparkling like an orchard of cherry trees after a rain shower. Joy will be yours. How do we open our hearts to this after so much pain and disappointment? We have lost many things as we've passed through the battlefields of this war-torn world; our humanity has been stripped of such essential goodness. One of our greatest losses is the gift of wonder, the doorway into the kingdom heart. But each of us has special places and favorite stories that are still able to reawaken it.

We love being taken into the homeliness of the hobbit's shire, but our hearts begin to race when Frodo learns he must flee and never return. Wonder grows as we push farther into the unknown realms—the Old Forest, the Inn of the Prancing Pony, the journey through the wilderness with a Ranger they know as Strider. Rivendell enchants, but that tang of dangerous adventure returns again when the fellowship sets forth on the quest upon which all Middle Earth depends:

> They crossed the bridge and wound slowly up the long steep paths that led out of the cloven vale of Rivendell; and they came at length to the high moor where the wind hissed through the heather. Then with one glance at the Last Homely House twinkling below them they strode away far into the night.[1]

Sometimes even a single phrase like "they strode away far into the night" can awaken in us a sense of longing that almost pierces. There are parts of us, no matter how deeply buried, that still remember we were made for this.

The hero in the movie *Avatar* is offered "a fresh start in a new world." I think that helps explain the film's wild success;

it still holds the global box office record, grossing more than $2 *billion*. To be honest, it is not the most remarkable story ever told; in fact, it is like every story ever told. The enchantment lies entirely with the fresh start the hero is given and the magical world itself, Pandora, a tropical Eden-like moon. It is a world straight out of a fairy tale, with wonders at every turn—islands that float in the sky, mythical beasts, flowers that glow at night then fly away when you touch them.

Narnia, Middle Earth, Pandora, Tatooine—they are all new worlds and yet not *entirely* new. There are trees and streams, deserts and animals like enough to our own world to be familiar, yet different enough to be enchanting. Chesterton believed this was the secret to romance—the blend of the familiar and new, "to be at once astonished at the world and yet at home in it."[2] He felt the reason every age still reads fairy tales is actually not to escape our world but to *re-enchant* it: "These tales say that apples were golden only to refresh the forgotten moment when we found that they were green. They make rivers run with wine only to make us remember, for one wild moment, that they run with water."[3] Or run with the water of life.

Our hearts long to recover a sense of wonder; it is one of the reasons only the child-heart can receive the kingdom. Remember now—we shall be as children again:

> "Let the little children come to me, and do not hinder them, for the kingdom of God belongs to such as these. Truly I tell you, anyone who will not receive the kingdom

of God like a little child will never enter it." (Mark 10:14–15)

The adult in us says, *How touching*, and dismisses it the next moment in order to go on with our very grown-up lives. But Jesus is being utterly serious, and thank God. For it is the child-heart still in us that loves Mos Eisley, Middle Earth, Narnia—these fairy-tale worlds that in hope-beyond-hope we long to be lost in ourselves. (Thus the allure of video games that let us do so, in an artificial way.) I believe it is right here that we can discern the longing for the kingdom most clearly—the child in us longing for wonder and a "new world"; the promise of the earth in its wildest and most radiant moments whispering back, *It is coming; it's just around the corner.*

This resurrection life you received from God is not a timid, grave-tending life. It's adventurously expectant, greeting God with a childlike "What's next, Papa?" God's Spirit touches our spirits and confirms who we really are. We know who he is, and we know who we are: Father and children. And we know we are going to get what's coming to us—an unbelievable inheritance! We go through exactly what Christ goes through. If we go through the hard times with him, then we're certainly going to go through the good times with him!

That's why I don't think there's any comparison between the present hard times and the coming good times. The created world itself can hardly wait for what's coming next. Everything in creation is being more or less held back. God reins it in until both creation and all the creatures are ready and can be released at the same moment into the glorious times ahead. Meanwhile, the joyful anticipation deepens. (Romans 8:15–21 THE MESSAGE)

"What's next, Papa?" indeed.

CREATION IS RESTORED

As a boy I loved all things new—a new book, a new bike, new cowboy boots; new lunch box, pocketknife, haircut, friend. Most adults love the "newness" of something new—the smell of a new car, the carpet in a new house. A new song, a new set of your favorite gear, new shoes (clearly Imelda's love was the newness of those shoes; she only wore them once, if at all). "New year, new you" goes the marketing every January. We all long for a fresh start in a new world.

And you shall have it. For, as we saw in chapter 2, God does not destroy the earth nor his beloved creation; he makes everything brand spanking new. Oh, the *wonder* of it!

I was walking in a grove of aspens yesterday evening. They are such beautiful, elegant trees—long white trunks, white as snow, grow upward fifty feet or more before the leaves crown the tops. I love the smoothness of the trunks, bending slightly here and there as they reach upward; there is something about their form that reminds me of the beauty of a woman's body.

At this time of year the leaves are golden, and the late sunlight coming through a forest of aspens turns golden as it passes through the canopy. A soft breeze was blowing, and the yellow leaves were fluttering gently down all around me, falling softly like flower petals. It felt like some heavenly benediction. Tall evergreens—spruces—were scattered in the grove of aspens, and the golden leaves caught on their green boughs and made them look like they were decked out for some holiday—like there was a grand party in the forest the night before.

Here among hundreds of living pillars of white crowned with gold, I understand why the Celts believed in the sacred groves. Just to place my hand on the smoothness of a trunk and feel its coolness and the life within, that is a healing act. The forest of white columns could have been a sanctuary from heaven or Lothlorien—the elven kingdom of Middle Earth.

When his eyes were in turn uncovered, Frodo looked up and caught his breath. They were standing in an open space. To the left stood a great mound, covered with a sward of grass as green as Spring-time in the Elder Days. Upon it, as a double crown, grew two circles of trees: the outer had bark of snowy white, and were leafless but beautiful in their shapely nakedness; the inner were mallorn-trees of great height, still arrayed in pale gold. . . .

The others cast themselves down upon the fragrant

grass, but Frodo stood awhile still lost in wonder. It seemed to him that he had stepped through a high window that looked on a vanished world. A light was upon it for which his language had no name. All that he saw was shapely, but the shapes seemed at once clear cut, as if they had been first conceived and drawn at the uncovering of his eyes, and ancient as if they had endured for ever. . . .

He turned and saw that Sam was now standing beside him, looking round with a puzzled expression, and rubbing his eyes as if he was not sure that he was awake. "It's sunlight and bright day, right enough," he said. "I thought that Elves were all for moon and stars: but this is more elvish than anything I ever heard tell of. I feel as if I was inside a song, if you take my meaning."[4]

Yes—all this shall be ours, a breathtaking world waiting right outside our door when all the earth is restored to its full glory. The return of Jesus may come with the trumpet blast, but what musical score will accompany the restoration of all things? Will it begin quietly, a single oboe, piercing and beautiful and poetic? Will it swell and crescendo to a mighty orchestra?

Perhaps you have walked by a pond or mountain lake and seen in it the reflection of the trees, meadows, and mountains, dappled, shifting, like an impressionist painting. Then you look up and see the real thing, the substance of it, the clear, shining reality of it all. It is not something "other," and yet it is more real, more true to itself. What do the fjords of Norway look like when they are completely unveiled? What of the Andes or the waters of the South Pacific? English painter Lilias Trotter burst into tears when she first saw the Alps, overcome by their beauty; will we weep or shout or stand speechless when we see them *reborn*?

Oh yes, we will recover wonder.

Stasi and I honeymooned in Yosemite National Park. We had never been in that majestic valley before, and we arrived late into the night, after a long drive, collapsing into bed with no idea whatsoever the cathedrals that rose all around us, the valley John Muir described as "extremely rugged, with its main features on the grandest scale in height and depth. . . . Benevolent, solemn, fateful, pervaded with divine light, every landscape glows like a countenance hallowed in eternal repose . . . pulsing with the heartbeats of God."[5] I woke in the morning a little groggy and stepped out the back door to have a stretch; thundering down thousands of feet before me roared Yosemite Falls. All I could do was yell, "Stasi! Stasi! Get *out* here!"

What will *waterfalls* be like in the new earth? What of the giant sequoias or tender wildflowers? What will rain be like? And think of your special places; imagine what it will be like to see them in their glory. How sweet it will be to revisit treasured nooks and vistas, gardens and swimming holes again, see them as they truly "are," unveiled, everything God meant them to be. Part of what makes the wonder so precious is that while it is a "new" world, it is *our* world, the world dearest to our hearts, romance at its best.

Including the Animal Kingdom!

I was in my office this morning, knees bent and body doubled over, so that my forehead almost touched the ground. I like that position as I pray. I find it very centering, comforting; it is almost fetal, primal. Suddenly a little furry muzzle and wet nose were pushing their way through my arm; our young golden had decided it was time to play. The intrusion was so startling and winsome, familiar and disruptive, I thought to myself, *What will it be like when a wolf pup does this . . . or a polar bear cub?*

For we will once again be lords of the earth with all creation coming to hand joyfully, eagerly, without fear.

The child-heart wants to know, "Will there be animals in heaven?" and the calloused grown-up heart dismisses the question as theologically unworthy. May I point out that the whole debate ends when you realize that heaven comes to *earth*; our home is right here on a renewed planet. How could our creative God renew his precious earth and not fill it with a renewed animal kingdom? That would be like a school without children, a village without people. The sheer barrenness and bleakness of the thought is utterly abhorrent to the child-heart of God and his love for the animals, his precious creations.

We know there are horses, for Jesus and his company return on horseback:

Then I saw Heaven open wide—and oh! a white horse and its Rider. The Rider, named Faithful and True, judges and makes war in pure righteousness.... The armies of Heaven, mounted on white horses and dressed in dazzling white linen, follow him. (Revelation 19:11–14 THE MESSAGE)

I wonder what Jesus named his horse. Does he come to his whistle? Does he need a saddle? I bet he rides bareback like the American Indians did. I've seen those horses, the cavalry of heaven, several times now. It happened as we brought the gospel on mission into foreign territory. We would be in a time of worship and suddenly I would "see" the front line of mounted horsemen spreading out before me like the Rohirrim before Gondor in *The Lord of the Rings*, pennants waving, row upon row of horse and rider behind, lifted spears like a forest. Oh yes—there are horses in the kingdom.

> The wolf will romp with the lamb,
> the leopard sleep with the kid.
> Calf and lion will eat from the same trough,
> and a little child will tend them.
> Cow and bear will graze the same pasture,
> their calves and cubs grow up together,
> and the lion eat straw like the ox.
> The nursing child will crawl over rattlesnake dens,
> the toddler stick his hand down the hole of a serpent.
> Neither animal nor human will hurt or kill
> on my holy mountain.
> The whole earth will be brimming with knowing God-
> Alive,

a living knowledge of God ocean-deep, ocean-wide.
(Isaiah 11:6–9 THE MESSAGE)

Now, unless you want to dismiss this as completely allegorical, we have wolves, lambs, leopards, goats, cows, lions, and bears in the kingdom as well. The passage is clearly describing the kingdom of God operating in its fullness on earth—the renewal of all things. And animals are clearly a part of it, praise our loving Father.

But this time around—I can barely write this without trembling—the animal kingdom will be our joyful partners. They will not be afraid of us anymore; they will long to love and serve us. For we were once lords of the animal kingdom, and in the re-created earth we shall take up that beautiful mantle again. What animals would you love to come to your call, to have a deep and holy friendship with? Even in this ailing world we see glimpses of what Adam and Eve must have enjoyed, in the lives of those men and women who seem to have a special gift with animals. Horse "whisperers" who with gentle wisdom are able to take a frightened and completely wild colt and within hours win its trust enough to ride it. The Mongolian shepherds who have trained golden eagles to hunt with them. The Indian men who work the timber forests with the help of elephants, riding them bareback and using only their knees to communicate.

Lawrence Anthony had a special relationship with African elephants; he authored a book called *The Elephant Whisperer: My Life with the Herd in the African Wild.* In 1999, he was asked to take charge of a dangerous group of elephants brought to his preserve, and over time they formed a sacred bond. Elephants have long been known to mourn the death of a member of their herd, but on the night of Anthony's death something very special took place. After traveling for more than twelve hours, two herds of elephants arrived shortly after his death, "where they appeared to stand vigil for two days."⁶ This is how the animals must have behaved back in Eden, honoring our First Parents, intuitively knowing their needs and we theirs.

Imagine the animals coming to our call, coming to honor us as their renewed masters. What will it be like to be partners again with nature?

And what does a *restored* rabbit look like? Is he bigger? Faster? Does he bound with greater leaps? What about a restored bear? The bears of this world grow larger the farther north you go; what is the size of a bear in its Eden-glory? Are restored bears more beautiful? Of course they are, and certainly gentle, for "neither animal nor human will hurt or kill on my holy mountain." Imagine—we will be like Noah, as the animals run to us to be reacquainted.

Will your childhood dog run to meet you? (God makes all things new.) Will he be taller, stronger, though every bit his true self? Will his bright eyes have so much to say? Think about the *intelligence* of restored creation. We are only now beginning to learn the true comprehension of animals. Your dog might not be cooperating, but canines understand more than 165 words (!); brain scans reveal that their minds process what we say and how we say it just like human brains do.[7] We know dolphins are extremely bright and playful; they employ a diverse language researchers call "extensive and complex."[8] Fully restored humans will have all the intuitive faculties and animal sense to communicate with a bright, intelligent, and restored animal kingdom. And the Holy Spirit will fill every relationship, enabling us to grow in perfect understanding of them and they of us. How could we be their shepherd lords again if we do not "speak" to one another?

My heart just skipped a beat. We are getting close to Narnia indeed. Or perhaps Narnia was simply peeking into the Renewal; I think it will be far more wondrous to "speak" to animals each in their language, rather than have them all speak ours.

PLAYING IN CREATION

I will devote a coming chapter to what our "work" will be in the kingdom, for we are said to "reign on the earth" (Revelation 5:10). Meanwhile, keeping in mind that it is our child-heart that receives the kingdom, let's dream about what it will be like to play in the remade world!

I am enchanted by the legends of ancient Polynesian cultures like the Maori and their tales of the "whale riders," mighty lords of old who had a bond so deep with nature they were able to ride on the backs of whales like we ride a horse or camel. Perhaps those legends are only mythic, but they speak of a wild and holy desire (there is the longing for the kingdom again). Or perhaps those legends were actually *prophecy*. We do see a small glimpse of this in the trainers who ride whales in theme parks. I am all for freeing Willy, but if that can happen in a fallen world, what lies before us in a world made young and innocent?

Creation *wants* to play. My dogs allow me about an hour and a half at the keyboard before they interrupt and insist on a romp. Perhaps you've had the joy of being on a boat in warm waters and seeing the happiness of the dolphins who come to surf the bow wake, making a deliberate choice to drop whatever it was they were doing and come to the sound, come to play on the fringes of our humanity. Nick Jans tells the story of a rare encounter with a black wolf in Juneau, Alaska, who came out of the woods one day on the outskirts of town and played with the dogs locals had brought to run there. Wildlife biologists consider one sighting in a lifetime a success. The wolf hung around for years, showing a keen desire to interact and even play with humans, as if he were a messenger from Eden.[9]

I saw horses and riders in the kingdom. What else might we ride? People currently ride elephants, water buffalo, ostriches, camels, orcas, giant tortoises—why shouldn't we play with all creation when we are reconciled, when happiness permeates every living thing and God himself is here among us? Of course we will swim with the whales, and in loving-kindness of course they will offer to take us on their backs. Yes, Revelation implies "there was no longer any sea"

(21:1). But many scholars believe this is alluding to the fact that the ancients, including the Jews, held the sea to be a habitation of evil. Of course evil is gone. But the earth cannot function without the oceans; they play a critical role in our water cycle, weather, and planet temperature. Besides—who can imagine a new earth without the glorious ocean?

Perhaps more importantly, the Greek of Revelation 21:1 speaks of one world "passing away" so that a remade world may take its place. Therefore Eugene Peterson in *The Message* translates the passage, "I saw Heaven and earth new-created. Gone the first Heaven, gone the first earth, gone the sea." Gone only in the sense of the old passing, so the renewed can take its place.

The eagles carried Sam and Frodo to safety; Gandalf rode them several times. *What if?* A large golden eagle in our world can lift a sheep and carry it away. What load can a renewed eagle bear? I would love to ride a golden eagle, with its permission of course. And, friends—I have not even mentioned the angels. Heaven comes to earth, and the angels shall walk in fellowship with man. What do the angels have to teach us? What sort of games do they play? The entire earth will be our playground. I see massive games like lacrosse being played by angels and men across vast landscapes.

This is why you don't need a bucket list. It's all yours, and you can never lose it. Oh, how I long to wander the beautiful places, without a curfew, without the end of vacation always looming. You've longed to see the fjords of Norway? Done. You've secretly hoped to wander the jungles of Africa? Yours too. What next? The Amazon? Antarctica? And I am only touching on the earth. What of the microscopic world? It is as vast as the world we call our own, and we shall explore its mysteries. What of the heavens? They, too, shall be ours. As Scottish poet George MacDonald wrote:

> I do live expecting great things in the life that is ripening for me and all mine—when we shall have all the universe for our own, and be good merry helpful children in the great house of our father. Then, darling, you and I and all will have the grand liberty wherewith Christ makes free—opening his hand to send us out like white doves to range the universe.[10]

Good thing we have all the time in the world that has no time to explore and come home and tell the tales. To take up new adventures with those who want to sail the seven seas or climb the peaks of the Andes or range the universe itself.

Remember—Jesus is the forerunner, the "second Adam." All that he was, we shall be. We will have restored bodies like the body of Christ after his resurrection—able to walk on water and defy certain limits known to us now. "St Peter for a few seconds walked on the water," wrote C. S. Lewis, "and the day will come when there will be a re-made universe, *infinitely* obedient to the will of glorified and obedient men, when we can do all things, when we shall be those gods that we are described as being in Scripture."[11] I love the picture he gave us of this very possibility toward the end of the Narnian tale *The Last Battle*:

———

It was the Unicorn who summed up what everyone was feeling. He stamped his right fore-hoof on the ground and neighed and then cried: "I have come home at last! This is my real country! I belong here. This is the land I have been looking for all my life, though I never knew it till now. The reason why we loved the old Narnia is that it sometimes looked a little like this. Bree-hee-hee! Come further up, come further in!" He shook his mane and sprang forward into a great gallop—a Unicorn's gallop which, in our world, would have carried him out of sight in a few moments. But now a most strange thing happened. Everyone else began to run, and they found, to their astonishment, that they could keep up with him. . . . The air flew in their faces as if they were driving fast in a car without a windscreen. The country flew past as if they were seeing it from the windows of an express train. Faster and faster they raced, but no one got hot or tired or out of breath. If one could run without getting tired, I don't think one would often want to do anything else. . . . So they ran faster and faster till it was more like flying than running, and even the Eagle overhead was going no faster than they. And they went through winding valley after winding valley and up the steep sides of hills and, faster than ever, down the other sides, following the river and sometimes crossing it and skimming across mountain-lakes as if they were living speedboats.[12]

You think I am being fanciful. I am being utterly serious. I am being as serious as Jesus when he warned that only the child-heart can receive the kingdom. Do you really want to suggest sinful man can create stories and worlds that outshine the worlds God will remake? Careful there. "No eye has seen, no ear has heard, and no mind has imagined what God has prepared for those who love him" (1 Corinthians 2:9 NLT). It was our creative Father who gave us our imaginations; the "visions" we tell in story are often prophetic glimpses into his wondrous realms, and his creative majesty will certainly do ours one better in the world to come.

WELCOMING THE PROMISE

I am treasuring now every taste of the promise that comes my way. I am seeking them out with new eyes, letting them broaden my kingdom imagination, fill these empty files with brilliant expectations.

Years ago, while visiting friends in Kauai, we discovered one of those moments that overflows with the wonder and allure of the coming kingdom. We had borrowed sea kayaks and come nightfall would paddle out in the dark, under the Pacific stars, out past the breakers into the rolling swells. The surf hits the reef a few hundred yards out from shore, and there was only one gap through which you could pass somewhat safely out into open water. And there we would sit, letting our pounding hearts calm, riding up and down on the rollers coming in, and just . . . letting it all take our breath away. The jet-black ocean beneath us, with who knows what swimming by; the night sky above, just as black and even deeper, allow-ing the stars to do their best; and often, the warm Kauai rain gently falling on us for a few minutes.

In a small kayak you feel everything—the currents, the swells, your own fragility. Out there in the dark it was like floating on the mystery of God—holy, mesmerizing, and more than a little unnerving. But the beauty and adventure were irresistible, and it became something we did every time we visited.

The currents move you up and down the coast, so as we began to paddle back in we searched in the dark for the one gap that would allow us to shoot through the crashing waves over the reef and into the lagoon. The luminescent foam allowed a glimpse of the place where the breakers weren't thundering onto the coral, and there we would catch the thrilling ride back in. Once past the reef, just inches below, the lagoon opened up quiet and calm; we felt safer from the sharks in there.

There are a few dozen cottages scattered along that stretch of beach and then dark cliffs behind. No hotels, no condo honeycombs; just the simple warmth of a few softly glowing porch lights calling you home. Paddling in felt like a moment from the kingdom.

These precious moments—so filled with the promise—are "hauntings" from the Spirit of God, given to us to lift our hearts into the wonder of the restoration of all things. And very soon we will visit those waters again and swim without fear at night, playing with the dolphins and whales, and then riding the waves themselves into the beach where we will sit around the campfires of the kingdom and tell stories late into the night.

The things we are discussing are utterly real, friends. Utterly real and the most concrete part of your future.

. . . until both creation and all the creatures are ready and can be released at the same moment into the glorious times ahead. Meanwhile, the joyful anticipation deepens. (Romans 8:18–21 THE MESSAGE)

There is a deep and holy connection between creation's release and ours. It waits upon us. Let's explore that next.

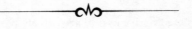

I had a dream about Craig a few nights ago.

I was at some sort of gathering, filled with people from our community. I'm not sure if it was an "earthly" event or a kingdom one. It felt simply ordinary.

But then again.

I looked to my right, and across the room I saw Craig. He was standing there talking to someone, as if he'd never been away.

In my dream I burst into tears. I've never done that in a dream before.

CHAPTER 5

Our Restoration

He knew something about growing up in a
motherless home, and about the hole it left in a boy's
heart. He knew about the ceaseless drive to make
oneself whole, and about the endless yearning.

DANIEL BROWN, *The Boys in the Boat*

I had a surprising emotional breakthrough the weekend my father died.

Like for many people, my relationship with my dad was kind of a mixed bag. My boyhood days were very precious. My father loved the outdoors, and we did a lot of camping and fishing together; I have golden memories of those days. But then the fall of man caught up with him: a series of lost jobs, followed by the drinking; then a stroke; then cancer; finally that brutal mocker, dementia. He spent his last days

---

in a small convalescent facility in Southern California, then came home for hospice.

He died on Father's Day weekend, of all sad things.

We'd been expecting it, living in those awful days of waiting that so often come at the end. Stasi and I had gone up to our cabin in the mountains; there is no phone service there, so I would drive the three miles down a dirt road to the highway, morning and evening to check in with my sister. On that Saturday morning when I reached cell service I saw there was a message; I decided to listen to it before calling her back. Sure enough—it was the call no one wants to get, explaining Dad had passed in the night.

I put the phone down and just sat in my truck in the early morning, waiting for the waves of grief, sorrow, and regret. So much had been lost; so much irrecoverable. The sun was just coming over the mountains, and the irrigation ditch was bubbling next to me like a brook; the meadowlarks called to one another across the lush hay fields. It was not a melancholy scene at all. As I gazed on the flowing water rippling over water grasses, I thought of a scene in *The Silver Chair*.

Toward the end of the story, the children sent to Narnia find themselves once again high on Aslan's mountain. King Caspian has died, and even though they have left that sad scene back on the quay, the funeral music is still somehow playing around them:

They were walking beside the stream and the Lion went before them: and he became so beautiful, and the music so despairing, that Jill did not know which of them it was that filled her eyes with tears.

Then Aslan stopped, and the children looked into the stream. And there, on the golden gravel of the bed of the stream, lay King Caspian, dead, with the water flowing over him like liquid glass. His long white beard swayed in it like water weed. And all three stood and wept. Even the lion wept: great Lion-tears, each tear more precious than the Earth would be if it was a single solid diamond. . . .

"Son of Adam," said Aslan, "go into that thicket and pluck the thorn that you will find there and bring it to me." Eustace obeyed. The thorn was a foot long and sharp as a rapier. "Drive it into my paw, son of Adam," said Aslan, holding up his right fore-paw and spreading out the great pad toward Eustace. "Must I?" said Eustace. "Yes," said Aslan.

Then Eustace set his teeth and drove the thorn into the Lion's pad. And there came out a great drop of blood, redder than all redness that you have ever seen or imagined. And it splashed into the stream over the dead body of the King. At the same moment the doleful music stopped. And the dead King began to be changed. His white beard turned to gray, and from gray to yellow, and got shorter and vanished all together; and his sunken cheeks grew round and fresh, and the wrinkles were smoothed, and his eyes opened, and his eyes and lips both laughed, and suddenly he leapt up and stood before them—a very young man. . . . And he rushed to Aslan and flung his arms as far as they would go round the huge neck; and he gave Aslan the strong kisses of a King, and Aslan gave him the wild kisses of a lion.[1]

This moment is yours, as sure and certain as God himself. Sure as the renewal of heaven and earth. How else could we enjoy the fierce beauty of a renewed creation unless we, too, are renewed and made strong, stronger than we ever were here? How could we possibly play in the fields of a new earth or fulfill our roles in the kingdom of God unless we are, well—glorious?

Forever Young

He wraps you in goodness—beauty eternal.
　　He renews your youth—you're always young in his presence. (Psalm 103:4–5 THE MESSAGE)

Death is utterly swept away at the Great Restoration. And not only death, but every other form of sorrow, assault, illness, and harm we've ever known. You will be completely renewed—body, soul, and spirit. How do we even imagine this? Take it in small steps; think of some recovery you have experienced. A piercing headache can be debilitating; you know the sweet relief when it vanishes. Surely you have had some nasty flu, and you know what a joy it was to get your strength and appetite back. These little glimpses of our restoration are taking place all the time, hints of what is coming.

Stasi came into the kitchen this morning with her running shoes on. I looked up with a surprised expression on my face. "Where are you going?" I asked. "I'm going for my walk," she said, as if it were the most natural thing in the world. Tears filled my eyes; I have not heard those words in a very long time. Walking has not been the most natural thing in the world for her. Oh, it once was. But it has been exactly one year since Stasi went for a walk.

Last fall she had an injury, tore her labral muscle in her right hip. That muscle provides the primary internal stability in the hip socket, and with it gone, deep arthritic erosion was revealed underneath. For the next nine months Stasi lived in chronic pain, bone-rubbing-on-bone pain, the kind only narcotics relieve. She walked with a cane when she walked at all; but most days she was confined to a chair. She lost her daily morning prayer walk, her precious time where she brings her heart back to the heart of God, prays for all those she cares so deeply about. Her prayer walk is her primary act of restoration in a stressful life. Hip surgery came in June; a summer of slow recovery followed.

So when she happily sashayed out the front door pain-free, I really could have fallen on the floor and wept for relief and joy. Such a simple thing, really, but in this hurting world physical restoration can feel like getting your life back. As the English poet George Herbert yearned,

Oh that I once past changing were

Fast in thy paradise, where no flower can wither.[2]

Many people face far, far worse. I think of the woman I helped in the grocery store last week. She was only in her thirties, I'm guessing, but she was bent over in her wheelchair, tiny and frail. A veil of shame and disappointment had permanently shaped her countenance; you have seen that tragic mask, I'm sure. I helped her reach the egg salad on the shelf above, but my heart broke for her. This is her life? What do you say to the soldier horribly maimed by stepping on an IED? What restoration awaits the woman who, due to a series of complications after surgery, lost three of her limbs and must be turned in bed many times a day?

Thank God we have more than empathy to offer; we have the restoration of Jesus to point to as a solid, vivid demonstration of our coming renewal.

The broken body of Jesus was horribly torn apart by his torture and execution; I wince even to write of it. "He didn't even look human—a ruined face, disfigured past recognition" (Isaiah 52:14 THE MESSAGE). But then, wonder of wonders, two mornings later he was completely renewed at his resurrection. Our Forerunner was physically restored and then some. Gone the thorn in his brow, gone the spear in his side, gone the nails in his hands. His body was beautiful and whole again. So great was his happiness he spent Easter in some very playful encounters with his friends.[3]

Praise the Lord, my soul;

    all my inmost being, praise his holy name.

Praise the Lord, my soul,

    and forget not all his benefits . . .

who redeems your life from the pit

    and crowns you with love and compassion,

who satisfies your desires with good things

so that your youth is renewed like the eagle's. (Psalm
      103:1–5)

Again—these promises are so beautiful our parched souls can hardly take them in, as the sunbaked earth can barely receive the thundershowers it so desperately needs. Just linger on this one promise for a moment—your loving Father will renew your youth. No one is old in his kingdom.

We are a golden retriever family; currently, we have two. Oban—our nine-year-old—is lying on the deck right now warming himself in the sunshine. He is, after all, sixty-three in dog years. With a raised eyebrow he is watching Maisie—our eighteen-month-old—who is into anything and everything in a matter of moments. Before I wrote this sentence she was chasing a bird; now she is digging a hole with earnest attention, fully convinced that if she digs hard enough she'll get that gopher; she looks up for a moment, tongue out, nose and face covered with dirt, eyes bright and head cocked as if to say, *Isn't this fantastic?!* A chipmunk races by, and she chases it with absolute joy, tail high like a flag; then it's back to rummaging around in the bushes. *Hey, look—here's my ball! Wanna play?*

When we hike she is always running past us, to the right and left, exploring. If we find water she is the first in; if it's snow then she'll slide down it on her back like a polar bear. Her joy is boundless; her *enjoyment* of everything is boundless. Because she is young. This will be our joy in the new earth, as we are made new.

Youth is what enables us to enjoy life. No, that's not quite right; *youthfulness* is what enables us to find the wonder in everything. Vibrancy. Lighthearted, like you feel late into a long vacation. Hopeful, like a child on Christmas morning. The absence of all cynicism and resignation—not to mention all physical suffering.

I love that part in *The Silver Chair* when old age simply vanishes from frail King Caspian, because age is the unavoidable meltdown, stripping even the bravest and most beautiful of their former glory. Whatever physical affliction you have known, whatever your limitations have been, everything old age will eventually strip you of—it will all be washed away. Your renewed body will be like the body of Jesus. We will burst forth into the new creation like children let out for summer break, running, somersaulting, cartwheeling into the meadows of the new earth. Running like the children, "without getting tired . . . faster and faster till it was more like flying than running, and even the Eagle overhead was going no faster than they."

OUR INTERNAL RESTORATION

"'He will wipe every tear from their eyes. There will be
no more death' or mourning or crying or pain, for the old
order of things has passed away."

He who was seated on the throne said, "I am making
everything new!" (Revelation 21:4–5)

No more tears. No more pain. No more death. No longer
any reason to mourn. At the renewal of all things, our hearts
are going to be free from grief. The joy of this will far surpass
our physical relief. Think of it—if God would offer today to
remove from you just one of your greatest sources of internal
pain, what would you ask him to remove?

And once it were gone, what would your joy be like?

Oh my goodness—I would be a happy maniac, dancing
in my underwear like David before the ark,[4] running about
the neighborhood like Scrooge on Christmas morning, leap-
ing housetop to housetop like the fiddler on the roof. And if
all your brokenness were finally and completely healed, and
all your sin removed from you as far as the east is from the
west[5]—what will you no longer face? What will you finally
be? How about your loved ones—what will they no longer
wrestle with? What do they finally get to be?

We shall, finally and fully, be *wholehearted*—a wish so
deep in my soul I can hardly speak it.

I was holding our new granddaughter the other night

on my knees, such a tiny and fragile thing. And my heart was pierced for her because I know what hell this world can unleash on a tender heart. The human heart and soul are imbued with a remarkable resilience. But they are also very fragile, for we were made for the habitat of Eden and not the desolation of war in which we now live. When the promised Messiah is foretold in Isaiah, the center of his work is clearly named—he will come to heal all our inner brokenness:

> The Spirit of the Sovereign LORD is on me,
>   because the LORD has anointed me
>   to proclaim good news to the poor.
> He has sent me to bind up the brokenhearted,
>   to proclaim freedom for the captives
> and release from darkness for the prisoners.
>   (Isaiah 61:1)

The Hebrew for "brokenhearted" is a conjunction of two words: *leb*, which is the heart, and *shabar*, a word that means "broken" or "to break, to rend violently." Isaiah elsewhere uses *shabar* to describe dry branches that are broken into pieces, or statues that have fallen off their pedestals and shattered upon the ground. *Shabar* refers to a *literal* breaking, the shattering of the human heart. As if I had to explain this to you; a tender and compassionate look into your own soul will show you exactly what I am talking about.

A good deal of research is coming forth to confirm what Isaiah described thousands of years ago: human beings are actually a collection of shattered "pieces." Dr. Bessel van der Kolk, one of the leading experts in trauma research, discovered after decades of inquiry that every person carries within themselves a shattered personality. What we see in dramatic form in dissociative identity disorder (DID—what used to be called multiple personality disorder), we all know to some measure ourselves. "As dramatic as its symptoms are, the internal splitting . . . as experienced in DID represents only the extreme end of the spectrum of mental life." In other words, we are fragmented beings. "We all have parts. . . . Parts are not just feelings but distinct ways of being, with their own beliefs, agendas, and roles in the overall ecology of our lives."[6]

You know the internal war this is describing.

It is the unhappiness and isolation of our inner parts that cause so much of the unrest, awkwardness, and sabotage in our lives. James describes the poor souls who are "like a wave of the sea, blown and tossed by the wind. . . . Such a person is double-minded and unstable in all they do" (1:6, 8). The Greek here for "double-minded" is *dipsuchos*, which is better translated "two-souled" or "split-souled." Did you just feel that inner tremor? Something in you is responding to this even as you read it. We are all traumatized and fragmented; no one passes through this vale of tears without it.

And our Healer will make us whole again. The little boy or girl in you who has so long hidden in fear, the angry adolescent, the heartbroken man or woman—all of "you" will be brought home to you, a fully integrated human being. "At such a time, we will be fully integrated once again—body, mind, spirit, and soul—just as we were intended to live with God at the beginning of creation."[7]

Think of it—to be wholehearted. To be filled with goodness from head to toe. To have an inner glory that matches the glory of your new body:

> The LORD their God will save his people on that day
>> as a shepherd saves his flock.
> They will sparkle in his land
>> like jewels in a crown.
> How attractive and beautiful they will be! (Zechariah
>> 9:16–17)

"Then the righteous will shine like the sun in the kingdom of their Father." (Matthew 13:43)

Think of a girl six years old at her dance recital. Imagine she has just given a splendid performance and she knows her mommy and daddy and grandpa are there watching. As she steps forward to receive her ribbon, her face is shining. She is radiant because she is *happy*. Think of a bride on her wedding day, in the joy after the ceremony and well into the reception. During the dancing someone snaps a photo, and afterward when you see it you are in awe of her countenance; she was shining because she was in her glory, loved, chosen, celebrated. "She was shining tonight."

And there is more.

You have come to Mount Zion, to the city of the living God, the heavenly Jerusalem, and to countless thousands of angels in a joyful gathering. You have come to the assembly of God's firstborn children, whose names are written in heaven. You have come to God himself, who is the judge over all things. You have come to the spirits of the righteous ones in heaven who have now been made perfect. (Hebrews 12:22–23 NLT)

That phrase "the righteous ones . . . made perfect." I can hardly speak. Finally, the totality of our being will be saturated only with goodness. Think of it—think of all that you're not going to have to wrestle with anymore. The fear that has been your lifelong battle, the anger, the compulsions, the battles to forgive, that nasty root of resentment. No more internal civil wars; no doubt, no lust, no regret; no shame, no self-hatred, no gender confusion. What has plagued you these last many years? What has plagued you all your life? Your Healer will personally lift it from your shoulders.

What tender intimacy is foretold when we are promised that our loving Father will wipe every tear from our eyes *personally*—not only tears of sorrow, but all the tears of shame, guilt, and remorse. That moment alone will make the whole journey worth it.

Yet there is more. The armies of heaven ride in on white horses, dressed in white linen. It is a symbol of the righteousness that now radiates from their hearts, the center of their being. The radiance is *character*; it is goodness. You will be free, alive, whole, young, gorgeous, valiant.

> Who knows how we'll end up! What we know is that when Christ is openly revealed, we'll see him—and in seeing him, become like him. All of us who look forward to his Coming stay ready, with the glistening purity of Jesus' life as a model for our own. (1 John 3:2–3 THE MESSAGE)

We will have the character, the internal holiness, of Jesus himself.

You will finally be everything you've ever longed to be. Not only that—it can never be taken from you again. "Eternal" life means life unending, life that never dims nor fades away. You will be in your glory to live as you were meant to live and take on the kingdom assignments God has for you. More on that in a moment. Let's stay with our restoration here.

Have you ever imagined what you would be like if the Fall had never taken place? Have you wondered what an unbroken, unstained, glorious, true, unblemished version of you would be? No false self, no woundedness, nothing shaped by the broken, mad world? No? Me neither. It is almost incomprehensible.

But you are going to get to know that person really well.

SEEING OUR LOVED ONES RESTORED

And those the LORD has rescued will return.
They will enter Zion with singing;
  everlasting joy will crown their heads.
Gladness and joy will overtake them,
and sorrow and sighing will flee away. (Isaiah 35:10)

What will it be like to have everlasting joy crown us? To be "overtaken" with gladness and joy? There is certainly the joy of *relief*. People who survive accidents often break out in giddy laughter afterward, relief overtaking the fear of the event. But there is also the joy of *anticipation*, the joy that comes when you know the road has opened before you and life will now happen the way you've always wished it would. Both shall be ours, the relief, followed by the thrill of anticipation—probably in that order.

It may be a difficult thing for you to imagine, your soul's complete restoration. But perhaps we can get there when we think of the restoration of the ones we love. Think of the joy it will be to see your spouse, your dearest friend, your son or daughter no longer fighting their internal battles. To see them young and well, alive and free, everything you knew they were! You always knew there was a radiance, a trueness, a shining greatness in there, though they never could quite take hold of it for themselves. And you *see* it. How many times over will we hear at the feast, "Look at you! You're glorious!"?

Stasi and I have dreams now and then about our parents

long departed. But in the dream we forget that they died years ago, and our reaction in the dream is, "Where have you *been*? It's been so long!" I stood at the window of Craig's office yesterday, looking at the boxes that remained, and wondered, *Where did you go?* I know where he is, but the heart has such a hard time with death (there's our longing for the kingdom again). Poet Stanley Kunitz asks, "How shall the heart be reconciled to its feast of losses?"[8] It is reconciled in great part as we behold with our own eyes the restoration of the ones we love. And it is reconciled through all the reunions that will take place.

Whom do you look forward to seeing again? We're all going to be at the wedding feast, for we are each of us guests of honor at that banquet. We get Bilbo's party. Put that on your bathroom mirror: *We get Bilbo's party!* Just think of the joy in all the reunions that will take place! I want to be there when Patrick jumps into his mother's and father's arms. Oh, to see again the ones we have lost and know they can never be taken from us again. After the tears of joy and the very long embraces, all those moments when we simply step back and say, "Let me look at you! My, how you've grown!"

After that . . . think of the storytelling!

Elie Wiesel said God created man because he loves stories. There will be so many stories to tell. "Where have you been?" "What were you doing?" All the questions that will finally have answers: "What actually happened when your lines were overrun by the enemy? It's wonderful to see you again, but I need to hear the rest of the story!" "Did you hear your daughter grew up to be a famous surgeon? Of course you did—you were probably involved in helping her pass her exams." And one question that particularly haunts me, for I know how much shrouds even the best relationship: "Did you know how much I loved you?"

I think the tales we get to both hear and tell at the party-over-the-water is also why we shall be "feasted." There's a lovely picture of this toward the end of the Narnian tale *The Horse and His Boy*:

> A grand feast [was] held that evening on the lawn before the castle, with dozens of lanterns to help the moonlight. And the wine flowed and tales were told and jokes were cracked, and then silence was made [for the telling of important tales]. Bree . . . told the story of the fight of Zalindreh. And Lucy told again . . . the tale of the Wardrobe and how she and King Edmund and Queen Susan and Peter the High King had first come into Narnia.[9]

Think of it—a hush comes over the wedding feast as certain guests are called forward to tell the Great Stories. Moses recounts the flight from Egypt and the parting of the sea. David comes forth to reenact his battle with Goliath. Mary steps forward (will she be clothed with the sun?) and tells stories from the hidden days of Jesus' boyhood. A murmur of excitement ripples through the crowd as Adam and Eve step forward and rather bashfully tell the story of naming the animals (they had a few disagreements that had to be sorted out over the hedgehog and the narwhal).

And no one will grow tired, no one will need to head off to bed. For we will be young, and whole, and filled with Life.

WONDER AND OUR HEALING

God heals the earth, and he heals us. We are restored to one another. The earth waits for our healing, and we wait for the earth's healing. I believe our healing brings about something of the healing of the earth (more on this in chapter 8), and I'm certain the healed earth helps to usher in our healing.

Our Enemy is the Great Divider. His most poisonous work takes place at the level of fragmentation, dividing families, churches, and fomenting racial hatred. He uses pain and suffering to create deep divisions within our own beings. You see his work right there, in the beginning of our tragic story, when he slithers into Eden to divide humanity from God, from one another, *and from the earth*. He traumatizes human beings, then separates them from the earth that could bring about their healing. In his highly researched book *Last Child in the Woods*, Richard Louv[10] documents how postmodern human beings suffer badly the physical and mental harms of "nature deficit disorder." Our lives have become cut off from the Garden we were meant to flourish in.

Children actually need to play in the dirt to develop some of the friendly bacteria the human body needs. Evidence is mounting that many immune deficiency disorders are actually caused because we live in too sterile an environment. A short walk in the woods reduces your cortisol stress levels. Isn't it sweet of God that sunshine gives us vitamin D; people always say how sunshine makes them happy. It actually does. Patients with windows looking out on nature recover at far higher rates than those who have no view. Nature heals, dear ones; nature heals. God has ordained that in the new earth it is *river* water that brings us life and *leaves* that are used for our healing:

> Then the angel showed me a river with the water of life, clear as crystal, flowing from the throne of God and of the Lamb. It flowed down the center of the main street. On each side of the river grew a tree of life, bearing twelve crops of fruit, with a fresh crop each month. The leaves were used for medicine to heal the nations. (Revelation 22:1–2 NLT)

Think of the sensual experiences of a restored you in a restored world. What will the aromas be?

Perhaps you've walked through a pine forest on a warm day; if you get up close to the bark, especially on a ponderosa, it smells like butterscotch. My grandmother used to put butterscotch on our ice cream. Can you imagine a whole forest filled with it? I remember the orange groves in Southern California in bloom—such a sweet and lovely scent. I expect the orchards near the city of God will wash the feast in lovely fragrances. My grandfather's ranch was situated in a valley where some folks grew fields of mint; the smell when they harvested was glorious, the whole valley smelled of mojitos or Christmas. We now understand more how fragrances actually affect the brain and facilitate healing. The aromas of the new earth will bring our healing too.

And what about the sounds of the new Eden? Even now the music of rushing water soothes my soul; I love to sit by babbling brooks, fall asleep to the sound of ocean waves. Just last night two owls were hooting back and forth to each other in our woods; it made my tired soul lighter somehow. We will hear nature in full chorus. It will mingle with the laughter and music and aromas of the feast itself, and we will wander in and out, drinking it all in, practically swimming in the healing powers of creation, feeling Life permeate every last corner of our being. Happiness and joy will overcome us; sorrow and its sighing will vanish forever.

I dreamed again of Craig. Has grief opened my soul like heaven's window?

He was standing in a crowd of people; rather, an assembly was standing around him. I know this time I was seeing the kingdom, for Jesus was there, standing before Craig as the witnesses drew around in a semicircle. It was a ceremony of some sort.

I saw Craig bow his head; Jesus placed over him a mantle or medallion, like we do the gold medal winner at the Olympics, or when the president awards the Medal of Honor. I felt like I was witnessing something very holy—a moment heaven especially loves.

When I began to relate the dream to a friend who also loved Craig deeply, he said—before he even heard the scene I wanted to describe—"It was his promotion, his rank in the kingdom." "Yes," I replied.

That same morning I received an e-mail from someone who knew neither of this conversation nor of my dream. The title of the e-mail was "Craig's promotion."

Jesus will go to great lengths to assure us when most precious things need assurance.

CHAPTER 6

When Every Story
Is Told Rightly

I long to hear the story of your life.

SHAKESPEARE, *The Tempest*

When J. R. R. Tolkien released his epic trilogy, C. S. Lewis was asked by a literary journal to write a review. He called the masterpiece "lightning from a clear sky . . . heroic romance, gorgeous, eloquent, and unashamed, has suddenly returned at a period almost pathological in its anti-romanticism."[1] *Pathological* is a strong word; I think Lewis would have chosen an even stronger one sixty years later. For we live in an age of staggering unbelief, a thoroughly deconstructed age where wonder has been stripped from everything. We no longer believe in the noble, the heroic, or the epic. The biggest part of our day is a latte from Starbucks or a funny YouTube video someone sends us.

For this reason I love the great stories and use them in my writing. They are the closest representation to the true nature of life in God's kingdom and the Story we find ourselves in. They are the rescue we need in order to see things clearly. When we are exhorted in Scripture to take up sword and shield, to "be on the alert, stand firm in the faith, act like men, be strong," it sounds quaint to our disenchanted ears.[2] But earlier saints were stirred to the marrow; the call to courage would have roused the deepest longings in them. Their imaginations would have drawn strength from tales of the great warriors of old.

Tolkien was deeply influenced by the epic poem *Beowulf*, written, as many believe, by a monk in the Middle Ages. It tells the story of an ancient Danish kingdom ravaged by an evil monster and the valiant warrior who comes to deliver them. Tolkien's kingdom of Rohan is practically a mirror image of the besieged realm in *Beowulf*, and to picture Heorot, the proud house of the shield-danes in which much of the story takes place, you only need to imagine Théoden's Golden Hall Meduseld. The poem speaks of a warrior culture in a heroic age long past, but the legend is Christian through and through.[3]

Hrothgar is a good king of the Danes, their "mighty prince." He builds his golden hall and peace reigns in the land. But terror finds a way to torment every age, in one form or another. "Then a powerful demon, a prowler of the dark" comes out of the swamps to terrorize the shield-danes and feast on the corpses of their best warriors. Night after night the monster Grendel attacks the fortress; the fear and trauma last more than a year:

> All were endangered; young and old
> were hunted down by that dark death-shadow
> who lurked and swooped in the long nights
> on the misty moors; nobody knows
> where these reavers from hell roam on their errands.
> So Grendel waged his lonely war,
> inflicting constant cruelties on the people,
> atrocious hurt.[4]

The tragic news reaches a mighty warrior across the waters to the north, in the kingdom of Geatland, now southern Sweden. Beowulf is the Christ figure in the story, a strong deliverer:

> There was no one else like him alive.
> In his day, he was the mightiest man on earth, high-born
> and powerful.[5]

Beowulf takes thirteen companions, fierce warriors, and comes to offer his help to the king of the Danes, who gratefully accepts. They feast together, then leave the hall to Beowulf and his warriors, knowing the demon will come again in the night to slake his unending bloodlust. Hrothgar warns Beowulf and promises a great reward:

Be on your mettle now, keep in mind your fame,
beware the enemy. There's nothing you wish for
that won't be yours if you win through alive.[6]

The beast does come and guts one of Beowulf's men before they even know he is upon them. What follows is one of the great battles in epic poetry, hand-to-hand combat between the foul demon and the Christ figure. Beowulf eventually delivers Grendel a mortal wound, and though the creature escapes to the moors, his doom is sealed. Then, in keeping with traditions that flow from ancient kingdoms right down to our own Medal of Honor, the hero is rewarded:

Then Halfdane's son presented Beowulf
with a gold standard as a victory gift,
an embroidered banner; also breast-mail
and a helmet; and a sword carried high,
that was both precious object and token of honor.[7]

The king orders eight horses with gold bridles be given to the hero, including the king's own horse and magnificent saddle.

The chieftain went on to reward the others:
each man on the bench who had sailed with Beowulf
and risked the voyage received a bounty,
some treasured possession.[8]

Of course the story does not end there. Grendel's mother, an even larger and more heinous creature, a "monstrous hell-bride," comes for revenge in the night, murdering the king's most beloved friend and counselor. Beowulf goes after her, and in a scene reminiscent of Christ descending into hell to wrench the keys from the Prince of Darkness, he descends into the swamp to slay Grendel's mother. The grateful Danes again reward him "with lavish wealth coffers of coiled gold."[9]

To the victor goes the spoils. The honor of scenes like this strikes some deep chord in the human heart, even those of us in an age that has lost all concept of honor and victory, of the high dignity of reward giving and receiving. Hrothgar is called "the grey-haired treasure-giver." It was common for kings to promise reward to their faithful, who would sacrifice so much, bear the heavy load, shed their own blood advancing the kingdom. David—the greatest of all Israel's kings—did so on many occasions.

REWARD

Now we are prepared to better understand Jesus. Let us return to that stunning passage with which we began our explorations of the *palingenesia*:

> "Truly I tell you, at the renewal of all things, when the
> Son of Man sits on his glorious throne . . . everyone who

has left houses or brothers or sisters or father or mother or wife or children or fields for my sake will receive a hundred times as much and will inherit eternal life." (Matthew 19:28–29)

Jesus was responding to a question when he declared these bold promises. The question came from Peter, though you get the feeling the other fellows put him up to it:

Then Peter said to him, "We've given up everything to follow you. What will we get?" (19:27 NLT)

Christ is neither alarmed nor offended by Peter's question. He doesn't tell him that service is enough, nor that virtue is its own reward. He quickly replies with the proclamation of the Great Renewal, and then—as though that were not enough (!)—goes on to assure the boys that they will be handsomely rewarded in the coming kingdom. A hundredfold. That's a pretty staggering return; perhaps Jesus is simply using hyperbole. But then there is his teaching on the minas and the talents:

"A man of noble birth went to a distant country to have himself appointed king and then to return. So he called ten of his servants and gave them ten minas. 'Put this money to work,' he said, 'until I come back.'

"But his subjects hated him and sent a delegation after him to say, 'We don't want this man to be our king.'

"He was made king, however, and returned home. Then he sent for the servants to whom he had given the money, in order to find out what they had gained with it.

"The first one came and said, 'Sir, your mina has earned ten more.'

"'Well done, my good servant!' his master replied. 'Because you have been trustworthy in a very small matter, take charge of ten cities.'

"The second came and said, 'Sir, your mina has earned five more.'

"His master answered, 'You take charge of five cities.'"
(Luke 19:12–19)

The allegory is hardly veiled. Clearly, Jesus is the man of noble birth who left to have himself appointed king (which took place at his ascension) and will return. Upon his return, he rewards his faithful servants (that would be us, his followers). He repeats the promise but ups the ante in the tale of the sheep and goats: "Come, you who are blessed by my Father; take your inheritance, the kingdom prepared for you since the creation of the world" (Matthew 25:31–36). We've gone from houses to cities to kingdoms. We are given *kingdoms*. Which helps to make sense of why we are said to reign with him. More on that in a moment. For now, can you see the theme here? The victorious king gladly rewards his faithful companions.

It is a mind-set almost entirely lost to our age. Who even talks about reward anymore? Who anticipates it? Expects it?

———

Honestly, I have never had one private conversation with any follower of Christ who spoke of their hope of being handsomely rewarded. Not once. Ever. This isn't virtue, friends; we have not exceeded the saints and Scripture itself in our humility. It is a sign of our complete and total bankruptcy.

REWARD IS A KINGDOM MIND-SET

Because our poverty is so great, it would do us good to let the repetition of Scripture open our eyes to how central reward is to a kingdom mind-set:

> "Rejoice and be glad, because great is your reward in heaven." (Matthew 5:12)

> "Be careful not to practice your righteousness in front of others to be seen by them. If you do, you will have no reward from your Father in heaven . . . But when you give to the needy, do not let your left hand know what your right hand is doing, so that your giving may be in secret. Then your Father, who sees what is done in secret, will reward you." (Matthew 6:1–4)

> "Store up for yourselves treasures in heaven." (Matthew 6:20)

> "Whoever welcomes a prophet as a prophet will receive a prophet's reward, and whoever welcomes a righteous person

as a righteous person will receive a righteous person's reward." (Matthew 10:41)

"For the Son of Man is going to come in his Father's glory with his angels, and then he will reward each person according to what they have done." (Matthew 16:27)

Serve wholeheartedly, as if you were serving the Lord, not people, because you know that the Lord will reward each one for whatever good they do, whether they are slave or free. (Ephesians 6:7–8)

Whatever you do, work at it with all your heart, as working for the Lord, not for human masters, since you know that you will receive an inheritance from the Lord as a reward. (Colossians 3:23–24)

So do not throw away your confidence; it will be richly rewarded. (Hebrews 10:35)

By faith Moses . . . chose to be mistreated along with the people of God rather than to enjoy the fleeting pleasures of sin. He regarded disgrace for the sake of Christ as of greater value than the treasures of Egypt, because he was looking ahead to his reward. (Hebrews 11:24–26)

The biblical canon ends with Jesus making this final statement:

———

"Look, I am coming soon! My reward is with me, and I will give to each person according to what they have done." (Revelation 22:12)

Reward, reward, reward—it fills the pages of both Testaments. Saint Paul expected to be rewarded for his service to Christ, as have the saints down through the ages. Patrick, that mighty missionary to the Irish, prayed daily, "In the hope of resurrection to meet with reward. . . . So that there may come to me an abundance of reward."[10] It is our barren age that is out of sync with the tradition. So C. S. Lewis could write,

> If we consider the unblushing promises of reward and the staggering nature of the rewards promised in the Gospels, it would seem that Our Lord finds our desires not too strong, but too weak. We are half-hearted creatures, fooling about with drink and sex and ambition when infinite joy is offered us, like an ignorant child who wants to go on making mud pies in a slum because he cannot imagine what is meant by the offer of a holiday at the sea.[11]

"The unblushing promises of reward" stopped me in my tracks the first time I read it many years ago. I've never heard a contemporary Christian use it. *Unblushing* means boldfaced, unashamed; it means brazen, outlandish, and thoroughly unapologetic. Did you know the promises of reward offered to you in Scripture are bold, unashamed, *brazen*? Did you even know that reward is a central theme in the teachings of Jesus, and in the Bible as a whole? I think a false humility has crept in; I think we somehow see ourselves above our forebears in the faith when we ignore the category entirely and set out to live the life given to us in Scripture. It is entirely untrue to the nature of God, and to human nature.

> Who serves as a soldier at his own expense? Who plants
> a vineyard and does not eat its grapes? Who tends a flock
> and does not drink the milk? (1 Corinthians 9:7)

God seems to be of the opinion that no one should be expected to sustain the rigors of the Christian life without very *robust* and *concrete* hopes of being brazenly rewarded for it. Now, yes, yes—there is a place for altruism, no doubt about it. But we have in our pride or in our poverty let a false humility creep in.

That pastor who serves a rather small, petty, and thank-less congregation for forty years, the man who works late hours visiting the sick and comforting the brokenhearted, the servant who is grossly underpaid and regularly berated by his own flock—what does he have to look forward to? Shouldn't his reception into the kingdom be like that of a great prince returning to his father's country, with lavish reward? Indeed, it will. Will not his kindness be rewarded? It will. Will not his longsuffering be rewarded? It will. In fact, every noble deed of his largely hidden faithfulness, every unsung and even misunderstood action of love will be *individually* and *specifically* rewarded (Matthew 10:41–42; 25:35–36). And so he shall be a rich nobleman in the kingdom of God. Everything he should have had but did not receive here will be his a hundredfold at the restoration of all things.

What about the believer who struggled under mental illness all her life, largely alone and almost completely misunderstood, clinging to her faith like a drowning woman clings to a rock while a broken mind tormented her daily? Should she not step into the kingdom like the queen of an entire country? Indeed, she will. She will probably be granted a position dispensing wisdom and insight that enriches the hearts and minds of her countrymen.

Oh yes, rewards will be given out in the kingdom with great honor and ceremony. And I believe one of our greatest joys will be to witness it happen.

When you think of all the stories of the saints through the ages, and all the beautiful, heroic, painful, utterly sacrificial choices made by those saints, the suffering, the persecution— how long will we enjoy hearing told the stories of those that ought to be rewarded, and then watch breathlessly as our King meets the specific situation with perfect generosity? The thought of it fills me with happiness even now. I have friends and loved ones for whom I want a front-row seat to witness this very moment.

In order for our lives to be rewarded, we need our stories to be told and told rightly.

———

YOUR STORY TOLD RIGHTLY

Victor Hugo's epic *Les Misérables* has obviously touched something deep in our humanity; there have been three different film versions and one massively successful Broadway musical done in my lifetime. I believe the enduring appeal of the story is that the promise is the overarching theme. The close of the musical and most recent film is an incredibly moving scene where all those who have died are back, singing the great anthem about how we will all be free and live in God's garden and every soul will receive their reward. It is a scene of the great *palingenesia*! No wonder the musical has been wildly popular.

But there is something else—the power of a story told rightly. Jean Valjean is such a good man, but fate has dealt him an unjust hand. He is a hunted man, misunderstood, maligned, having to flee one city to the next all his life. But *we* see his great heart, his sacrificial choices, and at the end we see he is finally vindicated—how he did the most loving and sacrificial thing, how his life was actually filled with beauty and dignity. The great cloud of witnesses shows up for his arrival into the kingdom of heaven and he deserves it.

Oh, how we ache for this moment, each one of us.

As we prepared for Craig's memorial service this summer, I was struck by the gross inadequacy of an hour or ninety minutes to meet the need. How do you tell the story of a human life? How can you do justice to all the hidden sorrow, the valiant fighting, the millions of small, unseen choices, the impact of a great soul on thousands of other lives? How can you begin to say what a life means to the kingdom of God?

The answer is, only *in* the kingdom of God. Only once we are there.

Your story will be told rightly. I know the idea has usually been set within the context of judgment and justice that will be served. But the friends of God do not face judgment; for us, the celebration of our lives is clearly put in the context of *reward*:

> But each one should build with care. For no one can lay any foundation other than the one already laid, which is Jesus Christ. If anyone builds on this foundation using gold, silver, costly stones, wood, hay or straw, their work will be shown for what it is, because the Day will bring it to light. It will be revealed with fire, and the fire will test the quality of each person's work. If what has been built survives, the builder will receive a reward. (1 Corinthians 3:10–14)

We know our every sin is forgiven; we know we live under mercy. We know there is no condemnation now for those who are in Christ (Romans 8:1). No condemnation, ever. We will be cloaked in righteousness, and it will emanate from our very being. So if we can remove all fear of exposure from our hearts, if we can set this safely within the context of our Father's love, it helps us toward a great, great moment in the kingdom: the time for every story to be told rightly.

———

How wonderful it will be to see Jesus Christ vindicated, after so many eons of mockery, dismissal, and vilification. Our Beloved has endured such slander, such mistrust, and, worst of all, such grotesque distortion by the caricatures and religious counterfeits paraded in his name. All the world will see him *as he is*, see him crowned King. Every tongue will be silenced, and his vindication will bring tremendous joy to those who love him!

But friends—that vindication is also yours.

You probably have a number of stories you would love to have told rightly—to have your actions explained and defended by Jesus. I know I do.

I think we will be surprised by what Jesus noticed. The "sheep" certainly are when their story is told: "Lord, when did we see you hungry and feed you, or thirsty and give you something to drink?" (Matthew 25:37). What a lovely surprise—all our choices great and small have been seen, and each act *will* be rewarded.

All those decisions your family misinterpreted and the accusations you bore, the many ways you paid for it. The thousands of unseen choices to overlook a cutting remark, a failure, to be kind to that friend who failed you again. The things that you wish you had personally done better, but at the time no one knew what you were laboring under—the warfare, the depression, the chronic fatigue. The millions of ways you have been missed and terribly misunderstood. Your Defender will make it all perfectly clear; you will be vindicated.

The Settling of Accounts

A few years ago my sons and I, with a few friends, fulfilled a longtime dream by making an adventure film about the gospel as an epic story. The film was set within the backdrop of a motorcycle trip we took through the wild lands of Colorado. The project was costly on every level; several riders were seriously hurt, and the spiritual warfare we endured was simply staggering. We poured our heart and soul into that project, hoping to present a winsome gospel to a new audience.

The backlash took us entirely by surprise. A vicious minority of the motorcycle community felt betrayed into watching a faith-based film and lashed out online with the hatred I spoke of in chapter 1. Vicious stuff, defamation, full-on cursing. My sons were repeatedly mocked online. It broke our hearts. The Christian community took their own shots, which added to our heartbreak. No one knew the full story.

Because it was faith-based we intentionally previewed the film to the leaders of the adventure-riding community and our sponsors, bike equipment companies. Everyone loved it; there was no indication the backlash was coming. And when it did come, cursing with all the fury of hell, we could not tell them their own people had been the ones to approve it (because we did not want to throw them under the bus, nor violate their kind support of us). No one came to our side. If they only knew the story, they would have known we did it all for the sake of their souls. The cost, the heinous warfare, the near death of one member—it was all for them.

Now, this is a small story among all stories, but one I can tell without incriminating someone specifically, and the cut is recent. It does my heart good to know that one day that story will be told rightly, and the vindication will be part of our healing. I'm not asking for revenge; I do not want to retaliate. Jesus is our defender. And, friends—Jesus *will* come to our defense. Your story needs to be told rightly. He won't let the injustices you have endured go unaddressed. That would be a violation of his nature and his kingdom. There are so many stories that need to be brought out into the light, and so much vindication that needs to take place if justice is real and healing true.

Frankly, there are a number of apologies I am looking forward to receiving.

And quite a few apologies I am looking forward to making myself.

There will be a day of reckoning. A settling of accounts. This was once central to the Christian view of the future, and absolutely critical to maintaining virtue in societies influenced by the church. Who even thinks like that anymore? How many transgressions large and small would be prevented if in that moment the perpetrator thought to himself, *I'm going to have to stand naked before Almighty God and explain this.* Fear of the Consuming Fire is perhaps the only thing the ungodly understand.

But for the *friends* of God, the settling of accounts is not meant to be negative at all; it is a great encouragement and sustaining hope! The vindication of our grievances, the honor given to our thousands of unseen choices, and the brazen promise of reward are intended to spur us on!

Envisioning Your Homecoming

So let me ask—what rewards are you looking forward to? I'm serious. Pause and think about it. What specific rewards are you banking everything on? Do you see how the entire concept lies empty in your soul, like an attic in an abandoned house? This place in your heart needs to be *filled* with rich images of real anticipation; this was meant to be the fuel that sustains your long journey here. Maybe the reason you have been losing heart is because you didn't know the great rewards that are just around the corner for you.

What do you want your reception in the kingdom to look like? Have you even thought about it?

Do you want to slide in by the hair of your chinny chin chin? There's a warning in Scripture about that. After Paul urges us to "build with care" in hopes of reward, he goes on to say that some people's lifework will be so shoddy it will be "burned up, the builder will suffer loss but yet will be saved—even though only as one escaping through the flames" (1 Corinthians 3:15). Just barely making it out of the burning house is not something to aspire to. I understand the gratitude of, "Look—I'm just grateful to be here." But we are urged on to so much more than that; to build carefully with a view of reward, to "run in such a way as to get the prize" (1 Corinthians 9:24).

Perhaps it is only a boyish desire (but remember, only the child-heart receives the kingdom), yet I love the stories where acts of courage are celebrated. Like Eustace's moment of honor in *The Voyage of the Dawn Treader*. Eustace has been more than obnoxious and wearisome; when he is turned into a dragon due to his own petty greed and pride, you feel he deserves it. But Aslan comes for him, and his salvation brings about a marvelous change of heart. Shortly afterward the ship is attacked by a sea serpent:

> Every man rushed to his weapon, but there was nothing to be done, the monster was out of reach. "Shoot! Shoot!" cried the Master Bowman, and several obeyed, but the arrows glanced off the Sea Serpent's hide as if it was iron-plated. Then, for a dreadful minute, everyone was still, staring up at its eyes and mouth and wondering where it would pounce. But it didn't pounce. It shot its head forward across the ship on a level with the yard of the mast. Now its head was just beside the fighting-top. Still it stretched and stretched till its head was over the starboard bulwark. Then down it began to come—not on to the crowded deck but into the water, so that the whole ship was under an arch of serpent. And almost at once that arch began to get smaller: indeed on the starboard the Sea Serpent was now almost touching the *Dawn Treader*'s side. Eustace . . .

now did the first brave thing he had ever done. He was wearing a sword that Caspian had lent him. As soon as the serpent's body was near enough on the starboard side he jumped up on the bulwark and began hacking at it with all his might. It is true that he accomplished nothing beyond breaking Caspian's second best sword into bits, but it was a fine thing for a beginner to have done.[12]

The ship just barely escapes the serpent's coils, and once they are free from danger Eustace is cheered for his bravery:

> But the *Dawn Treader* was already well away, running before a fresh breeze, and the men lay and sat panting and groaning all about the deck, till presently they were able to talk about it, and then to laugh about it. And when some rum had been served out they even raised a cheer; and everyone praised the valour of Eustace.[13]

A simple enough scene, but far better than the moment in *The Silver Chair* when the Great Lion looks upon Jill: "She knew at once that it had seen her, for its eyes looked straight into hers for a moment and then turned away—as if it knew her quite well and didn't think much of her."[14] Heavens no. Don't you want to be *cheered* at some point during the feast? "And everyone praised the valor of Nancy . . . of Brian . . . of Jennifer. Everyone raised their glass and cheered as their story was told rightly for the very first time." Of course you do. Even better still is a scene toward the end of *The Return of the King*, when dear Sam and Frodo—rescued from the fires of Mount Doom—have awakened to find themselves in the forest of Ithilien. Gandalf leads them through the beautiful woods toward the camp of Aragorn, now the king of Gondor:

> As they came to the opening in the wood, they were surprised to see knights in bright mail and tall guards in silver and black standing there, who greeted them with honour and bowed before them. And then one blew a long trumpet, and they went on through the aisle of trees beside the singing stream. So they came to a wide green land, and beyond it was a broad river in a silver haze, out of which rose a long wooded isle, and many ships lay by its shores. But on the field where they now stood a great host was drawn up, in ranks and companies glittering in the sun. And as the Hobbits approached swords were unsheathed, and spears were shaken, and horns and trumpets sang.[15]

Doesn't it bring tears to your eyes, knowing how much they have been through to deserve that moment? They more than deserve that moment, and it fills my own heart with longing for such a reception into the kingdom.

What would you love your reception into the kingdom to be? You should put some words to that, given how important it is.

A friend of mine who has labored long in the Great War

with evil shared his vision with me in a moment of tender vulnerability:

> I want to finish well. I want to return as a hero, a warrior worthy of the kingdom. I had this vision—I don't know if it was an actual vision or just my heart's expression. I saw myself, sword at my side, shield slung over my back, making my way up the main street of the City. I wore the battle gear of war, soiled by long years at the front. People lined both sides of the street to welcome me, the great cloud, I guess; I recognized hundreds of faces, the faces of those whose freedom I fought for. Their smiles and tears filled my heart with profound joy. As I made my way up the street toward Jesus and our Father, my friends and fellow warriors stepped into the street with me, and we moved forward as a band. I saw angels there, maybe the angels who fought for us and with us, walking alongside. I saw flower petals on the pavement; I saw banners flapping in the breeze. We reached the throne and knelt. Jesus came forward and kissed my forehead, and we embraced deeply, freely, like I always knew we would. Then my Father stepped forward and took me by the shoulders and said, "Well done, my son. Very well done indeed. Welcome home." As we embraced, a great cheer went up from the crowd.

Now, that would be a reception worth living for. The reality that every story will be told rightly should affect your choices today. If there is no cost to our Christian faith, how then shall we be rewarded? And may I point out that if we, too, would love to receive a hero's welcome, it helps to keep in mind that valiant deeds require desperate times. The desperate times are all around us, friends; now for the valiant deeds.

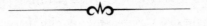

The promise came again this morning, on a very hard day.

Today is Patrick's due date, Sam and Susie's little boy. We would have held him in our arms; there would have been baseball games and birthday parties, ice cream and skinned knees and sleepovers. I would have read my favorite books to him. Losing Patrick was not simply a miscarriage. It meant losing an entire story.

He has gone before us, and we won't see him until the kingdom.

I was standing at the window again this morning, quietly mourning. The heavens began a light rain, like the tears of God. It wasn't supposed to rain today. How kind.

But then—very unexpectedly—the sun came out while it was still raining. Golden light shone through every falling raindrop, illuminating millions of drops, turning a gray, dismal moment into something magical, a shower of diamonds.

God had come to remind me again of everything promised in the Renewal.

CHAPTER 7

The Overthrow of Evil

"Gandalf! I thought you were dead! But then I thought I
was dead myself. Is everything sad going to come untrue?
What's happened to the world?" "A great Shadow has
departed," said Gandalf, and then he laughed and the
sound was like music, or like water in a parched land;
and as he listened the thought came to Sam that he
had not heard laughter, the pure sound of merriment,
for days upon days without count. It fell upon his ears
like the echo of all the joys he had ever known.

J. R. R. TOLKIEN, *The Lord of the Rings*

O nce upon a time the earth was whole and beautiful,
shimmering like an emerald, filled with glory, bursting
with *anticipation*. Such wonders waiting to be unveiled, such
adventures waiting to be ours. Creation was a fairy tale, a
great legend—only true.

Once upon a time we were whole and beautiful too, glorious, striding through the Garden like the sons and daughters of God. A daughter of God is a goddess; a son of God is a god. "I said, 'You are "gods"; you are all sons of the Most High'" (Psalm 82:6). We were holy and powerful; we ruled the earth and animal kingdom with loving-kindness.

But Eden was vulnerable; something dark slithered in the shadows. Something most foul and sinister. Banished from heaven, Satan and his fallen warriors came seeking revenge:

> To waste his whole Creation, or possess
> All as our own, and drive as we were driven,
> The punie habitants, or if not drive,
> Seduce them to our Party, that thir God
> May prove thir foe, and with repenting hand
> Abolish his own works. This would surpass
> Common revenge, and interrupt his joy
> . . . when his darling Sons
> Hurl'd headlong to partake with us, shall curse
> Thir frail Originals, and faded bliss,
> Faded so soon.[1]

If the coming Restoration is to be fulfilled on the earth and in our lives, Satan and his armies must be destroyed. He must never be allowed in again.

We are letting the great stories awaken our imaginations to the coming kingdom, fill our hearts with brilliant images and hopeful expectation. Let us seize the moment crucial to the climax of every story and the redemption we long to see: that glorious moment when evil is defeated.

Whether as children or adults, many of us fell in love with Aslan, the noble Christ-lion of Narnia. We can't forget that terrible scene when the White Witch drives the dagger into the Great Lion's heart with such evil relish.

> She stood by Aslan's head. Her face was working and twitching with passion, but his looked up at the sky, still quiet, neither angry nor afraid, but a little sad. Then, just before she gave the blow, she stooped down and said in a quivering voice, "And now, who has won? Fool, did you think that by all this you would save the human traitor? Now I will kill you instead of him as our pact was and so the Deep Magic will be appeased. But when you are dead what will prevent me from killing him as well? And who will take him out of my hand then? Understand that you have given me Narnia forever, you have lost your own life and you have not saved his. In that knowledge, despair and die." The children did not see the actual moment of the killing. They couldn't bear to look and had covered their eyes.[2]

A heartbreaking scene for every child-heart, young and old. If we did not know the end of the story it would be unbearable. How much greater our joy, then, when the *resurrected* Aslan leads his army to victory and avenges himself upon the Witch:

———

There stood Peter and Edmund and all the rest of Aslan's army fighting desperately against the crowd of horrible creatures whom [Lucy] had seen last night; only now, in the daylight, they looked even stranger and more evil and more deformed. There also seemed to be far more of them. Aslan's army—which had their backs to her—looked terribly few. And there were statues dotted all over the battlefield, so apparently the Witch had been using her wand. But she did not seem to be using it now. She was fighting with her stone knife. It was Peter she was fighting—both of them going at it so hard that Lucy could hardly make out what was happening; she only saw the stone knife and Peter's sword flashing so quickly that they looked like three knives and three swords. That pair were in the centre. On each side the line stretched out. Horrible things were happening wherever she looked.

"Off my back, children," shouted Aslan. And they both tumbled off. Then with a roar that shook all Narnia from the Western lamp-post to the shores of the Eastern sea the great beast flung himself upon the White Witch. Lucy saw her face lifted towards him for one second with an expression of terror and amazement.[3]

At last. At last. Doesn't something deep in your being resonate with this moment? *Please, Lord, yes. Vanquish evil. Make it soon.*

There are many moments of righteous justice in the long

battle with darkness Tolkien so powerfully portrays in his Rings trilogy. One of my favorites (Hollywood seized on it too) takes place on the Pelennor Fields during the last great battle for Middle Earth, when brave Éowyn destroys the witch king of Angmar, terror of men, leader of the Nazgul. That foul prince of darkness is about to unmake her lord and king, who has fallen:

Out of the wreck rose the Black Rider, tall and threatening, towering above her. With a cry of hatred that stung the very ears like venom he let fall his mace. Her shield was shivered in many pieces, and her arm was broken; she stumbled to her knees. He bent over her like a cloud, and his eyes glittered; he raised his mace to kill.

But suddenly he too stumbled forward with a cry of bitter pain, and his stroke went wide, driving into the ground. Merry's sword had stabbed him from behind, shearing through the black mantle, and passing up beneath the hauberk had pierced the sinew behind his mighty knee.

"Éowyn! Éowyn!" cried Merry. Then tottering, struggling up, with her last strength she drove her sword between crown and mantle, as the great shoulders bowed before her. The sword broke sparkling into many shards. The crown rolled away with a clang. Éowyn fell forward upon her fallen foe. But lo! the mantle and hauberk were empty. Shapeless they lay now on the ground, torn and tumbled; and a cry went up into the shuddering air, and faded to a shrill wailing, passing with the wind, a voice bodiless and thin that died, and was swallowed up, and was never heard again in that age of this world.[4]

You'll find this moment in nearly every story you love. Sometimes at the movies I can't help but yell out, *"Yes!"* when it happens. It's a little embarrassing, but I can't contain myself—not so much because of the story I'm watching, but because of the Day I am longing for with every fiber of my being.

Our Story

We love the fall of the Nazgul leader because it echoes this scene from our story:

> Satan will be released from his prison and will go out to deceive the nations in the four corners of the earth—Gog and Magog—and to gather them for battle. In number they are like the sand on the seashore. They marched across the breadth of the earth and surrounded the camp of God's people, the city he loves. But fire came down from heaven and devoured them. And the devil, who deceived them, was thrown into the lake of burning sulfur, where the beast and the false prophet had been thrown. They will be tormented day and night for ever and ever. (Revelation 20:7–10)

A moment of silence, please.

Pause and let this be true: evil is judged and utterly destroyed. Forever and ever. Not just in the fairy tale, but here in reality, in our Story. Satan, his armies, and every form of evil are destroyed with a punishment that never ends, under justice unrelenting.

It feels like a ten-ton weight being lifted off my being.

What will it be like to no longer be assaulted? To be utterly free from accusation; to look in the mirror and hear no accusing thoughts or voices. To be completely free of all temptation and the sabotage of your character—not because you are successfully resisting it in a moment of great resolve, but because it is *no longer in existence*, anywhere in the world. What will it be like to have the dark clouds lifted between us and our beloved Jesus, that veil that so often clouds our relationship with him? Imagine when all the physical affliction, emotional torment, abuse—all the evil in this world has vanished.

Think of it—what evils will you no longer have to live with personally?

Oh, the joy we will experience when we get to watch with our own eyes the Enemy brought down for good, cast into his eternal torment! Oh, the hope that begins to rise at the thought of a world where the Enemy no longer gets to do what he does. To see our loved ones released from their lifelong battles. To be released from our own lifelong battles, knowing with utter surety that the kingdom of death and darkness is forever destroyed.

This is my favorite scene in the film *The Last of the Mohicans*, a story set in the French and Indian War of the mid-1700s. It was a vicious war, with savagery practiced on both sides. In the film the archvillain is a very twisted character, the Huron Indian named Magua. His mind and heart are so tormented with bitterness and bloodlust, he gives himself over to become wickedness incarnate. Magua is a betrayer and murderer; he destroys the lives and happiness of many people.

The Mohawk warrior Chingachgook is the father figure in the film, like our heavenly Father. He has two sons— Uncas, his son by birth, and Nathanial, his adopted white son. Late in the film Magua has cut out the heart of an English captain and taken his two daughters as slaves; the daughters are each the love of one of Chingachgook's sons. (The bride taken captive, just as in our story.) The three warriors, father and sons, race to rescue them. Uncas reaches Magua first, but Magua is powerful; he kills the beautiful young Indian warrior and throws him off a cliff. His love, Alice, throws herself off behind him rather than become Magua's sexual slave. Then the father arrives and takes his revenge. Magua is brought down; Chingachgook kills him with his battle-ax.

The evil one finally gets what he deserves; he is stopped, judged, and destroyed. Every time I see a scene like that, I remind Satan that this is his end. *This is coming*, I think. *This is your end.*

You long for this day, and you long for it in very particular ways.

A HEART FOR REDEMPTION

Some stories and images stay in your mind for years; sadly, it is usually the darker ones. I remember leafing through a catalog of WWII photos when I came across one I could not stop looking at. At first all I saw was a large group of soldiers milling about; then I realized they were standing in a few long lines, smoking and chatting like soldiers waiting to get into the mess hall or use the latrine. I looked down at the inscription, which explained this mob of Japanese soldiers was waiting their turn with Korean "comfort girls," young captive women forced to have sex with hundreds of enemies every day.

I nearly threw up; I could even now as I tell you this. I wanted to scream; I wanted to do something about it.

The human race has showed itself capable of unspeakable evils at war. But war is now at our doorstep, and this practice has become a major global industry. Millions of human beings—including children—are forced into sexual acts every day on this planet; $186 billion is spent on prostitution worldwide annually.[5] Friends of mine who minister to the victims report that the stories they are hearing now are far more heinous than they were even ten years ago.

What does your heart do with that? What does your soul do hearing the stories of boys and girls trafficked into sexual torment? Just last week I heard another, from a Christian woman who confided she was sold by her mother to men starting at age six. She would hide under their kitchen table, but her mother would turn her over and leave the house while she was raped. What do we do with such evil that fills our world every single day? Do we not cry out for justice? Do you not feel more and more every day like poor Lot, who "was tormented in his righteous soul by the lawless deeds he saw and heard" (2 Peter 2:8)? You know the torment of living in an evil age; it is traumatizing to the soul. How long, O Lord, how *long*?

Now read this passage:

> After this I saw another angel coming down from heaven. He had great authority, and the earth was illuminated by his splendor. With a mighty voice he shouted:
>
> "'Fallen! Fallen is Babylon the Great!'
> She has become a dwelling for demons
> and a haunt for every impure spirit,
> a haunt for every unclean bird,
> a haunt for every unclean and detestable animal.
> For all the nations have drunk
> the maddening wine of her adulteries.
> The kings of the earth committed adultery with her,
> and the merchants of the earth grew rich from her
> excessive luxuries." (Revelation 18:1–3)

Human sin is not sufficient to explain the rampaging, unspeakable evil of this age. There are powerful, ancient dark spirits—those same fallen angels who invaded Eden—who are now deeply involved ensnaring, entrapping, fueling evil people, making war on holiness and on the human heart. The Whore of Babylon is the one behind the sex trade in all its dark corruptions; Scripture says she has made the world "drunk [with] the maddening wine of her adulteries" (Revelation 18:3). Truly, an intoxicated sexual madness has come over the earth. And she is going to be severely judged by our righteous Lord:

> "Give back to her as she has given;
>> pay her back double for what she has done.
>> Pour her a double portion from her own cup.
> Give her as much torment and grief
>> as the glory and luxury she gave herself.
> In her heart she boasts,
>> 'I sit enthroned as queen.
> I am not a widow;
>> I will never mourn.'
> Therefore in one day her plagues will overtake her:
>> death, mourning and famine.
> She will be consumed by fire,
>> for mighty is the Lord God who judges her."

"When the kings of the earth who committed adultery with her and shared her luxury see the smoke of her burning, they will weep and mourn over her. Terrified at her torment, they will stand far off and cry:

> "'Woe! Woe to you, great city,
>> you mighty city of Babylon!

In one hour your doom has come!'"
(Revelation 18:6–10)

This passage fills me with such relief, anticipation, and something like holy revenge. Think of every little girl and boy forced to have sex with corrupt adults; think of every woman and man drugged and held captive as sexual slaves. Think of the *shattering* of those human hearts. Now think of the shout that will go up when the Whore is cast down forever:

After this I heard what sounded like the roar of a great multitude in heaven shouting:

"Hallelujah!
Salvation and glory and power belong to our God,
 for true and just are his judgments.
He has condemned the great prostitute
 who corrupted the earth by her adulteries.
He has avenged on her the blood of his servants."

And again they shouted:

"Hallelujah!
The smoke from her goes up for ever and ever."

The twenty-four elders and the four living creatures fell down and worshiped God, who was seated on the throne.

And they cried:

"Amen, Hallelujah!"

Then a voice came from the throne, saying:

"Praise our God,
    all you his servants,
you who fear him,
    both great and small!"

Then I heard what sounded like a great multitude, like the roar of rushing waters and like loud peals of thunder, shouting:

"Hallelujah!
    For our Lord God Almighty reigns.
Let us rejoice and be glad
    and give him glory!
For the wedding of the Lamb has come,
    and his bride has made herself ready.
Fine linen, bright and clean,
    was given her to wear." (Revelation 19:1–8)

Won't it be marvelous to hear that roar of rushing waters, the triumphant shout like thunder from the hosts of the kingdom? You will hear that shout, friends; you will join it with all the power of your lungs.

———

And I have named only one evil. Think of all the justice that needs to be served. You have a heart for redemption. Your kingdom heart longs for restoration and reconciliation, for justice, for the recovery of all that has been lost. What is the redemption that your heart longs for on a global level? What passions arouse your heart? Is your heart for a people group? A community or nation? For the arts or sciences? You have very particular passions for justice and redemption, and they will be realized. Your heart needs to know this—they *will* be realized.

The children of Israel were seduced by many evil powers. That ancient spirit Molek somehow—how was it possible?—compelled them to sacrifice their own children:

> "They built high places for Baal in the Valley of Ben Hinnom to sacrifice their sons and daughters to Molek, though I never commanded—nor did it enter my mind—that they should do such a detestable thing and so make Judah sin." (Jeremiah 32:35)

This, too, has become a global industry. I can hardly bear to think of an entire industry devoted to killing children in the holy sanctuary of their mothers' wombs. No doubt it is fueled by Molek still, and Molek *will* be judged, just like the Whore; this heinous crime *will* end.

And what is the redemption your heart aches for on a personal level—for your family, your friends? What cries fill your prayers in the night? Oh, to see the day that alcohol no longer holds a family line in its grips, when abuse no longer tears a family apart. Nor poverty, nor shame, nor mental illness. You have very special and particular longings for redemption for those you love. And, my dear friends—those longings were given to you by the God who shares them, and they, too, *will* be fulfilled.

> Can plunder be taken from warriors,
> > or captives be rescued from the fierce?
>
> But this is what the LORD says:
>
> "Yes, captives will be taken from warriors,
> > and plunder retrieved from the fierce;
> I will contend with those who contend with you,
> > and your children I will save.
> I will make your oppressors eat their own flesh;
> > they will be drunk on their own blood, as with
> > > wine.
> Then all mankind will know
> > that I, the LORD, am your Savior,
> your Redeemer, the Mighty One of Jacob."
> > (Isaiah 49:24–26)

The promise of justice fulfilled is one of the great hopes of the coming kingdom.

JUSTICE WILL BE SERVED

We preach a gospel of mercy. But it is mercy bought at a terrible price. We are saved from the judgment of God, not because he decided to toss justice in the gutter, but because he poured it out upon his own Son on the cross. That mercy is being extended to all mankind—so long as we are in *this* age. But when the Day of the Lord arrives, justice will be served. A day of reckoning is coming, and we need it to be so.

Few of us may have made it through the 618 pages of Alexandre Dumas's *The Count of Monte Cristo*, but many of you have seen the movie. The story centers around the betrayal and injustice suffered by an innocent man, Edmond Dantès. Falsely accused of treason by a treasonous French official, Edmond flies to the home of his best friend, Fernand Mondego, who out of envy and jealousy betrays Dantès to the police. He is sentenced to the island prison Château d'If, where he is tortured for fourteen years. Edmond escapes, thanks to the priest, and thanks to the priest he recovers the fabulous treasure that allows him to become the Count of Monte Cristo.

Late in the story, at the climax of the film, Dantès confronts Mondego while Edmond's lifetime love and their son stand by. Edmond has every reason to take Mondego's life, but instead offers him a chance to repent. Mondego refuses. Edmond gives him a chance to flee. But when Mondego will not relent in doing evil, when he tries to take Edmond's life, Edmond kills him in a sword fight, and rightly so. There is a time for justice to be served. Even mercy has its limits.

This is where Hinduism, Buddhism, and other religions that deny or ignore the actual, personal existence of evil fall so short. (Branches of Christianity have done the same.) Without naming evil for exactly what it is, and without a day of reckoning, there can be no justice.

Imagine, friends, a world without evil. Every demon has been swept away. I will say more about who shares in the Great Restoration in chapter 9, but for now simply imagine a world without evil people, where everyone loves God and overflows with his holy love. You look to your right and left, and you only see people you can trust completely. Lot's torment will no longer be ours; holiness will permeate all things. No wonder joy is the constant mood of the kingdom! Not to mention massive relief and vindication too.

Our age cries out for justice, especially the younger generations. I believe in those justice movements; I support them. But I fear a great heartbreak is coming unless we understand the timing of things. Until the evil one is bound and cast into the lake of fire, our efforts here will be only partially successful. "The poor you will always have with you" (Matthew 26:11). A dear, dear man just e-mailed me; he and his wife run an orphanage for abused and trafficked girls in Guatemala. He aches because he has to turn away girls every week. They simply have no room to take them all in. This is a terrible reality: our best efforts *must* be carried on, but they will not achieve justice on the earth until our Lord's return.

I can hardly bear it; how do we carry on?

Only with the anchor of the soul; only with the sure and

firm hope that this Day is coming. Justice *is* coming. Those at the forefront of the justice movements must have the *palingenesia* before them daily.

OUR LONGING WILL BE FULFILLED

I have till this moment skipped over an important part of the passage where Jesus announces the *palingenesia*, the Great Restoration. Now is a good time to pick it up:

> Jesus replied, "Yes, you have followed me. In the re-creation of the world, when the Son of Man will rule gloriously, you who have followed me will also rule." (Matthew 19:28 THE MESSAGE)

"You who have followed me will also rule." We rule with Jesus. In the next chapter we will be unpacking that extensively, for it has to do with our roles in the new creation. But here we are speaking of the administration of justice when the evil one and all in his service are sentenced; I believe we have a role to play in that. We will be there when our Lord judges the evil that has oppressed our family. We will be called forward as witnesses for the prosecution. We will preside with him when justice is carried out on the evil that has been behind those causes dear to us—poverty, abuse, racism, human trafficking, and the destruction of the earth itself.

Intimate and personal justice will be granted to us as well.

You have suffered very specific wrongs over the course of your life; God is fully aware of every one of them. Jesus your King will make sure they are addressed with very specific reparations. Far be it from God to make light of it. "If anyone causes one of these little ones—those who believe in me—to stumble, it would be better for them to have a large millstone hung around their neck and to be drowned in the depths of the sea" (Matthew 18:6). He is furious about what you have endured, and he *will* make it right.

I know that so much has been stolen in my life. So many blessings, so many gifts, so much taken from my relationships, opportunities, personal restoration that was diminished or thwarted. You have too, dear ones—so much has been stolen from you. And it will be repaid a hundredfold. This recompense, this restitution must be part of telling every story rightly, or justice will not be fulfilled. And it *will* be fulfilled:

> "Then you will look and be radiant,
> > your heart will throb and swell with joy;
> the wealth on the seas will be brought to you,
> to you the riches of the nations will come." (Isaiah 60:5)

Imagine—after your enemies are judged and banished, great treasure chests are then brought in and set before you. Huge oak chests; it requires two men or angels to bring each one in, and there are several. Jesus tells you to open them. You ask, "What are these, Lord?" and he replies, *These are the gifts I meant for you in your former life but were stolen or prevented from making it to you. I return them now, with interest.* Imagine all that fills those chests. You hear laughter coming from one, for so much of what has been lost are memories and joy. I am weeping as I write this.

Then you turn to your right and ask, "And what are these chests, Lord?" *These are the rewards for your life's choices, your victories, your perseverance, and your service. In addition to your estates, of course,* he says with a smile.

Those treasure chests are yours, friends; their contents will thrill your heart and redeem so much of what you have endured here. Justice shall be yours, justice personal and particular. Wrongs will be avenged, hurts shall be healed, and all that was stolen from you in this life will be recompensed far beyond your wildest hopes. You will open those chests, look, and be radiant. Your heart will throb and swell with joy.

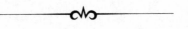

I dreamed about the city of God last night. This has been the most surprising vision of all, for I confess—I don't like cities. I have never been particularly moved when reading passages about "the city of God" or "the new Jerusalem."

But this city was unlike any I've ever seen; none of the crowding, the grinding noise, the sooty concrete. None of the industrial inhumanity.

What I saw was more like a Mediterranean city—whitewashed buildings, winding walkways, stairs leading up to open doorways. Everything had an elegant, curving whimsy to it. All windows and doors were arched; there were many domed roofs. Architecture as poetry, soothing to the soul. The place was filled with a soft light. It reminded me of pictures I've seen of the beautiful Greek island of Santorini or the Old City of Jerusalem. But of course.

It was enchanting in ways I have never experienced on earth. Each winding path made so many turns—ascending and descending stairs, coming suddenly upon fountains and court-yards, with any number of possible doors and gateways leading off—it was the sort of place you would want to explore for a long time.

But what most captured me was the laughter I heard within those bright rooms. Laughter kind and playful, gentle and true; laughter like it was the native tongue of the place.

CHAPTER 8

What Do We Actually *Do*?

Each mortal thing does one thing and the same. . . .
Crying Whát I dó is me: for that I came.

GERARD MANLEY HOPKINS,
"AS KINGFISHERS CATCH FIRE"

E vil is gone. The world is restored. *We* are restored. Justice has been served, and we are lavishly rewarded. The only natural thing to do, the only appropriate thing to do at that point, is pop a cork, open a cask, push back the furniture, and throw a riotous party! Of course we all head off to celebrate at a feast; I have no doubt it carries on for weeks, probably months! There are quite a few stories that need telling, and many reunions that must take place.

Then what? What do we do *after* the wedding feast of the Lamb?

———

Honestly, I think this is as far as most people have ever given it thought.

If we do talk at all about the joy of the coming kingdom, we talk about the feast, and nothing more. Our imaginations seem to end right there, falling off the edges of the banquet like ancient sailors feared they would fall off the end of the world. I am looking forward to the gala, for sure, but at some point the feast comes to a close, and just as every newly married couple drives away from their reception, we then have the rest of our unending life before us. What do we *do* with it?

This is probably the one aspect of our future most shrouded in religious vapors, fogged in by a pea soup of vagueness, emptiness, and heavenly foam—what is it that we *do*? When my dear friend Brent died, a few folks wanted to use a song at his service; because of its country-western style and religious message, it seemed to them to fit the bill perfectly. The refrain speaks of a man whose task on earth is finished and so he rests in peace high up on a mountainside. Now, I happen to like the work of Vince Gill. But I loathed this song then, and I loathe it still—*because* of its charming religious appeal and grotesque message. Your life is over; go rest now. Forever. This is the best we can come up with when it comes to eternal living? No wonder life here seems far more exciting. (And life here seems far more exciting for the vast majority of people— witnessed by the fact that no one you know is fantasizing about heaven.)

You will wake one morning and the earth will be made new.

On that same wonder-filled morning you will also be made new.

What adventures then unfold? What great tasks are set before us?

I'm not sure if it was the graceful, mesmerizing movements of the gazelle and impala, or the fierce presence of lions nearby, or the majesty of the elephant, but I will never forget the look on my daughter-in-law Susie's face, a look so rare in this world—the shining countenance of childhood wonder, eyes wide and glistening, mouth agape and smiling. She was utterly captivated as the rose-colored lights of sunrise revealed the vast array of animals and dancers while music itself swelled to match the scene.

We were in London watching the musical *The Lion King*. Surely you've seen the movie; the opening number is worth watching again this week to help your imagination seize the new earth with both hands. As the sun rises on the African savannah and flocks of birds soar overhead, God's menagerie of fantastic creatures assembles to honor their new prince. The scene is borrowed straight from Genesis, the morning of creation, when all the angels sang for joy. It is a moment when music is *required*, fitting hand in glove with creation (you'll remember Aslan sang Narnia into being). The opening song begins, heralding the moment of our birth and how each one of us steps blinking into a dazzling world filled with more than can possibly be seen or done in a lifetime.

Exactly. Precisely. Couldn't have said it better myself. More to see than can ever be seen, more to do than can ever be done *unless* you have all the time in a world without time to see it and to do it. Well then. We haven't begun to scratch the surface of the mysteries of the earth, haven't seen or experienced a fraction of this world, our home. What joys await us, what adventures call? This would be a far better song to sing at funerals; that is, if we also explained that our dear ones are in no way dead at all, that they will be right there with us when the new sun rises on the new earth. We should all stand and sing for the morning of re-creation.

The Excitement Has Only Just Begun

The next chapter of our story is precisely that—the chapter that *follows* all the chapters before and fits them perfectly. God is still telling a story; the next chapter is not disconnected from the rest. (I know it feels totally disconnected, but it is not.) If we will look at our future in light of the story God *has been* telling, it will banish the fog like a strong summer sun. Let's start with Genesis, the first Eden:

> "Let us make human beings in our image, to be like us. They will reign over the fish in the sea, the birds in the sky, the livestock, all the wild animals on the earth, and the small animals that scurry along the ground."

> So God created human beings in his own image.

In the image of God he created them;
male and female he created them.

Then God blessed them and said, "Be fruitful and multiply.
Fill the earth and govern it. Reign over the fish in the sea,
the birds in the sky, and all the animals that scurry along the
ground." (Genesis 1:26–28 NLT)

Our powerful and creative Father makes us in his image—
powerful and creative sons and daughters. He gives us the
earth like a wedding present, instructs us to reign, and endows
each human being with talents and gifts to carry out that task.
Father, Son, and Holy Spirit also included in the earth a latent
potency—veiled powers and treasures, things like music and
literature and science "hidden" in creation like Easter eggs
so we might have the joy of discovering them. "Hey—look
at this! I'm starting to put some things together, and I think
it's called 'music.' There are notes and chords, meter, and if
you stretch a string just right it makes a perfect C! Isn't this
incredible?!"

Think of the potential that was waiting in the first Eden
for glorious men and women to discover.

The long story of human history then follows, filled with
glory and tragedy. God's children prove themselves capable of
marvelous works; we also prove ourselves capable of terrible
deeds. Evil ravages the earth and the human race. Things go
from bad to worse until our loving Father intervenes; Jesus
Christ comes to overthrow the evil one and ransom us. He

begins the healing of our lives; he gives each of us a role in the church's great mission.

In the *next* chapter, our powerful and creative Father *re*-creates us and the earth. He then tells us to do exactly what he told Adam and Eve to do: *reign*. "You have made them to be a kingdom and priests to serve our God, and they will reign on the earth" (Revelation 5:10). Do you follow the story? Do you see the exciting connection? Glorious men and women are once again given a glorious world in order to do the very things it is in our nature to do. Only this time around with far greater powers, magnificent even. We have within *us* a latent potency, talents and gifts unrealized, soon to be made new; the renewed earth will be even more responsive to our leadership than the first time around. So Dallas Willard invites us to use our God-given imagination:

> We should think of our destiny as being absorbed in a tremendously creative team effort, with unimaginably splendid leadership, on an inconceivably vast plane of activity, with ever more comprehensive cycles of productivity and enjoyment. This is the "eye hath not seen, neither ear heard" that lies before us in the prophetic vision (Isa. 64:4).[1]

What will you do in the coming kingdom?

The simple, stunning answer is, *you will do everything you were born to do.*

ALL THINGS NEW

Up till now I have been speaking almost exclusively of the renewal of creation—the earth in all its splendor and the animal kingdom. I did so to help us grasp that we get our beautiful world back; it is also my attempt to wipe away the religious fog regarding heaven. However, at the epicenter of the renewal of all things is a *city*. And not just any city—it is the city of God, his very own home where he makes his dwelling with mankind.

> And I saw the holy city, the new Jerusalem, coming down from God out of heaven like a bride beautifully dressed for her husband.
>
> I heard a loud shout from the throne, saying, "Look, God's home is now among his people! He will live with them, and they will be his people. God himself will be with them. . . .
>
> "Come with me! I will show you the bride, the wife of the Lamb."
>
> So he took me in the Spirit to a great, high mountain, and he showed me the holy city, Jerusalem, descending out of heaven from God. It shone with the glory of God and sparkled like a precious stone—like jasper as clear as crystal. The city wall was broad and high, with twelve gates guarded by twelve angels. And the names of the twelve tribes of Israel were written on the gates. There were three gates on each side—east, north, south, and west. The wall

of the city had twelve foundation stones, and on them were written the names of the twelve apostles of the Lamb.

The angel who talked to me held in his hand a gold measuring stick to measure the city, its gates, and its wall. When he measured it, he found it was a square, as wide as it was long. In fact, its length and width and height were each 1,400 miles. (Revelation 21:2–3, 9–16 NLT)

A massive, stunning, glorious place, whose presence allows us to think about the renewal of the arts and sciences, education, and the trades. The promise is that God will make not "some things new" but *all things new.*

Begin with the obvious—we know there is music in the kingdom. Just think of what the music will be! The intimate and the grand; music played on a single violin, music played by a massive orchestra and choir. Drums. A capella voices. Think of all the talented musicians who dwell there! We get to hear the work of the great composers, played by their own hand. We will hear the angels sing in their own tongues as well. I expect the city will be filled with music; I'm sure we will be dancing on the tables. Follow me now—but who *makes* that music? Who makes the instruments upon which that music is played?

You do, my friends. At least, those of you who want to will. I'd love to learn to play the cello; it's always been one of my favorite instruments. I'd love to let loose on some taiko drums too. We're not just talking organ and choir here, for all the ethnic music from around the world will dwell in that place and joyful hearts will want to make music day and night. I wonder what instrument Jesus plays. I wonder what our Father's voice sounds like, how far it carries. (You will hear your Father sing!) Oh my. The thought of it brings me such happiness.

I would love to learn other languages—and won't it be wonderful that every tribe and tongue is there to teach us? Speaking of learning, imagine the scope of education in the city! Jonathan Edwards believed that learning will be one of the great pleasures of the kingdom. He pointed out that though we are resurrected, we are still finite beings. I doubt very much that God would simply "dump" all knowledge into us the moment we arrive. We grow and develop in the kingdom by learning, with renewed and strengthened minds filled with the Holy Spirit. Imagine taking philosophy from Thomas Aquinas or any of the great thinkers from the ages; Pascal perhaps (though he might be busy teaching math). Saint Paul will hold classes on the Torah; Galileo will give lectures on the stars. Oh, the joy of it!

I expect we will study history under the very figures who lived in those eras (Moses and Elijah appeared to chat with Jesus on the Mount of Transfiguration, which was a glimpse into the kingdom). Lincoln will teach classes on the Civil War, and Churchill will retell the Battle of Britain. I'm not quite sure how imagination and memory come together to honor history; perhaps we will "see it" as it is being told by those who lived it. Perhaps we will go further and *enter into it*—for all times are accessible to our glorious God, and he keeps all times within himself. There is no question those stories and episodes will be accessible to us somehow, and vividly.

Think of the sciences in the kingdom! Inquiry and discovery are essential if we would reign over creation—and by the way, the implication of a renewed "heavens" includes the universe. I mentioned earlier that we will be able to explore the microscopic world, which is as vast a universe as the one above us. All that there is yet to know, all that this precious knowledge will allow us to develop as friends share and build on the revelations given to us about the created order. The combustion engine will seem a crass and primitive thing to the great minds in the kingdom. What new glories are waiting to be discovered? Wonders leading to wonders leading to creative breakthroughs only imagined in science fiction on this side.

And what of the trades? We know we have homes and dwellings in the kingdom—who furnishes those homes? Who makes the chairs, the tables, the tapestries? I've always wanted to work with my hands. I would love to have the time and skill and mentors to build boats with hand tools and sail them, learning to navigate by the stars. Again, I am not being fanciful; I am utterly serious. You are healed and restored as a human being, with all the faculties of personhood given to you by God. So the question is, what have you always dreamed of doing? What gifts have you yearned to express? What have you always wanted to be great at? These things are part of your personhood; they are how God created you, and they will be even more glorious in the *re*-created you. Dream, my friends.

What have you watched someone else doing and longed to do as beautifully as they can? That is another way of accessing the hidden dreams and capacities in your own soul. Perhaps you've watched someone amazing at architecture, or teaching, horsemanship, physics, cooking, or engineering, and something in you leapt, longing to do the same. Well, there you go—that is part of your personhood and will be released into fullness in the kingdom.

As a boy I was taken many summers to the Oregon Shakespeare Festival. I vividly remember marveling (there's the wonder again) at the stage, sets, and costumes, the beautiful lighting under the stars. The skill of the actors and directors, the artistry of the entire production made my heart ache. I longed to be a Shakespearean actor, and though I realized a bit of that dream as a young man, I had to put it away, as many of us have had to put our dreams away in this life. Imagine *theater* in the kingdom! The joy of watching will be second only to the joy of those offering it.

Certainly storytelling is one of the great pleasures in the kingdom. God clearly takes it very seriously—he made reality in the shape of a story. Would you like to write? Illustrate? Act? Produce? Perhaps we get to take workshops from the great artists! These things are not obliterated when we step into the life to come; God renews *all* things. Willard assures us,

> We will not sit around looking at one another or at God for eternity but will join the eternal Logos, "reign with him," in the endlessly ongoing creative work of God. It is

for this that we were each individually intended, as both kings and priests (Exod. 19:6; Rev. 5:10). . . . A place in God's creative order has been reserved for each one of us from before the beginnings of cosmic existence. His plan is for us to develop, as apprentices to Jesus, to the point where we can take our place in the ongoing creativity of the universe.[2]

Just as Adam and Eve were commissioned to, only this time around on a higher level, with greater powers, creatively engaged in very real and tangible things. We know we eat in the city; surely the joy of eating doesn't end with the feast. Who grows the food? Who brings it to market? What chefs prepare it? It is unlike God to just "zap" these things into existence while we sit around doing nothing, bored to death. He creates us to create. Jesus linked the promise of the Restoration directly to familiar things like fields and lands, confirming the earlier prophetic visions of the Old Testament:

> "See, I will create
>> new heavens and a new earth.
> The former things will not be remembered,
>> nor will they come to mind.
> But be glad and rejoice forever
>> in what I will create,
> for I will create Jerusalem to be a delight
>> and its people a joy.
> I will rejoice over Jerusalem

and take delight in my people;
   the sound of weeping and of crying
      will be heard in it no more. . . .
   They will build houses and dwell in them;
      they will plant vineyards and eat their fruit." (Isaiah
        65:17–19, 21)

I would love to own and work my own vast vineyard! I'd love to try my hand at the wine-making process (and some even stronger things).

City Life, Country Life

Then the angel showed me a river with the water of life, clear as crystal, flowing from the throne of God and of the Lamb. It flowed down the center of the main street. On each side of the river grew a tree of life, bearing twelve crops of fruit, with a fresh crop each month. The leaves were used for medicine to heal the nations. (Revelation 22:1–2 NLT)

This is an actual river, flowing through an actual city. Its waters are crystal clear and flowing with life; liquid life flowing as a river. Growing on the banks of that river are real trees; their roots go down to drink those waters of life (which is probably why they are the trees of life). I *adore* rivers; they are high on my list of "favorite things." I love trees too. It makes me so happy to know that even in the city there are rivers and trees, and doubly happy that we find our healing in them, from them. Imagine the great parks in the city!

I wonder what colors the fruits of the tree of life are; are they different each of the twelve months? What does that queenly fruit taste like? Will it be something entirely new? Or will it taste like all your favorite childhood flavors almost tasted—your mother's blackberry pie, chocolate, vanilla ice cream—because the promise was coming through them to your child-heart? They'll be delicious, I have no doubt. And how large are those trees? They heal nations, so they must be magnificent—tall as redwoods, spreading as great banyan trees.

And how have you pictured the river? Subdued and delicate? Rather small, more like a canal? The Thames is almost three hundred yards across as it flows through London; ships navigate it. The Nile is almost a *mile* wide in Cairo. For some reason our famished imaginations picture the River of Life as more of a stream. Do we only drink from the river, respectfully dipping our cup? Or do we get to wade in it? Swim in it? Come on now—you will be standing on the banks of a river flowing with the water of *life*. You've been working up a thirst for that water *all* your life. I'm diving in.

The river flows through the city, but then it must flow out into the countryside. Do fly fishermen get to fish its waters at that point? Do families picnic on its banks on Sunday afternoons? We will soon find out. For I believe those who love the city life will find their joy in the city, and those who love the agrarian life will find their joy in the country. Both are promised in the coming kingdom:

> "I will make rivers flow on barren heights,
> and springs within the valleys.
> I will turn the desert into pools of water,
> and the parched ground into springs." (Isaiah 41:18)

> They will rebuild the ancient ruins
> and restore the places long devastated;
> they will renew the ruined cities
> that have been devastated for generations. (Isaiah 61:4)

This reminds me of one of my all-time favorite short stories: *The Man Who Planted Trees* by Jean Giono. The lovely little tale describes the anonymous life of a humble shepherd who transforms an entire countryside by planting trees in a wasteland. The story begins with the narrator—a young man at the time—taking a trek on foot through the rough hills of rural France.

> And after three days walking, [I] found myself in the midst of unparalleled desolation. I camped near the vestiges of an abandoned village. I had run out of water the day before, and had to find some. These clustered houses, although in ruins, like an old wasp's nest, suggested that there must once have been a spring or well here. There was indeed a spring, but it was dry. The five or six houses,

roofless, gnawed by wind and rain, the tiny chapel with its crumbling steeple, stood about like the houses and chapels in living villages, but all life had vanished.[3]

I've seen many such places myself, as I'm sure you have. He could be describing many villages in the war-torn Middle East, or the former Soviet bloc, or the abandoned farms and townships of the American West. Every time I drive by one of these abandoned places, I am struck with sadness over the fall of man and the ravages of evil; they make me long for the Great Renewal.

Farther on, the traveler comes across a shepherd, who invites him to stay the night in his little stone house. Before bed, the quiet peasant carefully selects one hundred perfect acorns from a pile on his table and puts them in a sack. Next morning, as he goes to the fields, he soaks his sack in water. The traveler follows the shepherd to see what this curious man is up to.

There he began thrusting his iron rod into the earth, making a hole in which he planted an acorn; then he refilled the hole. He was planting oak trees. I asked him if the land belonged to him. He answered no. Did he know whose it was? He did not.

For three years he had been planting trees in this wilderness. He had planted one hundred thousand. Of the hundred thousand, twenty thousand had sprouted. Of the twenty thousand he still expected to lose about half. . . .

There remained ten thousand oak trees to grow where nothing had grown before.[4]

The narrator is then called away to the terrible life of an infantryman in the First World War; amidst that carnage he entirely forgets the shepherd. After demobilization, he understandably finds himself with "a huge desire to breathe fresh air," so he sets out again through the barren lands. He again finds the shepherd, still at his work.

> The oaks of 1910 were then ten years old and taller than either of us. It was an impressive spectacle. I was literally speechless and, as he did not talk, we spent the whole day walking in silence through his forest. In three sections, it measured eleven kilometers in length and three kilometers at its greatest width. When you remembered that all this had sprung from the hands and the soul of this one man, without technical resources, you understood that men could be as effectual as God in other realms than that of destruction.[5]

Time passes; the peasant shepherd continues at his work, adding beech and birch trees to his reforestation efforts. In 1945, the narrator goes to see this quiet saint for the last time. He almost doesn't recognize the countryside; it has been utterly transformed.

> Everything was changed. Even the air. Instead of the harsh dry winds that used to attack me, a gentle breeze was

blowing, laden with scents. A sound like water came from the mountains: it was the wind in the forest. . . .

On the site of the ruins I had seen in 1913 now stand neat farms, cleanly plastered, testifying to a happy and comfortable life. The old streams, fed by the rains and snows that the forest conserves, are flowing again. Their waters have been channeled. On each farm, in groves of maples, fountain pools overflow on to carpets of fresh mint. Little by little the villages have been rebuilt. Counting the former population more than ten thousand people owe their happiness to [the humble shepherd].[6]

I do not know if Jean Giono intentionally created a parable of Isaiah's restoration prophecies, but "the ancient ruins" have been rebuilt and "the places long devastated" have been restored. Rivers "flow on barren heights, and springs within the valleys." The desert has been turned to pools of water, "and the parched ground into springs." I love this little tale for that reason, for the model of perseverance, and for the illustration of a life devoted to making the world a more beautiful place. Giono's redemption parable ends with this line:

When I reflect that one man, armed only with his own physical and moral resources, was able to cause this land of Canaan to spring from the wasteland . . . I am taken with an immense respect for that old and unlearned peasant who was able to complete a work worthy of God.[7]

We are each created to accomplish a work worthy of God; it is one of our deepest yearnings. And we will, in the kingdom; not just once, but many, many times over. Are we employed in the actual restoration itself? I don't know for certain. "They will rebuild the ancient ruins and restore the places long devastated" certainly hints at it. And we know our God is a God of *process*—look at how long your sanctification is taking.

You might think I am merely daydreaming about what we actually do in the kingdom. But, friends—God creates us to be creators like he is. We are promised we will reign; we will be given estates; we are told we will have vital roles in the coming kingdom.

> "After a long absence, the master of those three servants came back and settled up with them. The one given five thousand dollars showed him how he had doubled his investment. His master commended him: 'Good work! You did your job well. From now on be my partner.'" (Matthew 25:19–21 THE MESSAGE)

Come and "be my partner"—that's the perfect way to put it. The idea behind the parable is *promotion*. And notice that the servants are promoted in the very things they are good at! God puts his renewed sons and daughters—creators like he is—in a re-created world and tells us to do exactly what he told Adam and Eve to do in the beginning. N. T. Wright therefore says,

In Revelation and Paul's letters we are told that God's people will actually be running the new world on God's behalf. The idea of our participation in the new creation goes back to Genesis, when humans are supposed to be running the Garden and looking after the animals. If you transpose that all the way through, it's a picture like the one that you get at the end of Revelation.[8]

HITTING YOUR FULL STRIDE

We haven't yet seen anyone in their true glory. Including you.

Yes, Mozart did start writing symphonies as a child, and Picasso could draw before he could talk. But most human beings are profoundly thwarted in their "calling" here because of wounding, assault, envy, or circumstances that would never let them fly. For most human beings on this planet, work ranges from disappointing to oppressive. What does the kingdom offer those men who work the Indonesian sulfur mines or the tens of millions of modern slaves upon the earth? This is not what God intended. How many Mozarts are there right now, hidden in slums and huts across the globe?

All your creativity and gifting will be restored and then some when *you* are restored. All of that latent potency inside of you—so damaged here, marred, frustrated, never given the opportunity to grow and develop and express itself—all of it completely restored, including your personality. From there you are able to act in the new world in ways far greater than

Adam and Eve were able to act the first time around (and look at what humanity has been able to do with "be fruitful . . . rule" [Genesis 1:28] in a broken world!). You will have absolute intimacy with Jesus Christ, and his life will flow through your gifts unhindered. Imagine what we will be capable of, how vast our powers in the new earth! We know we shall walk on water, for Peter did on this earth at Jesus' bidding. How far do our creative and artistic capacities reach?

> When we are in our home, our natal home,
> When joy shall carry every sacred load,
> And from its life and peace no heart shall roam,
> What if thou make us able to make like thee—
> To light with moons, to clothe with greenery,
> To hang gold sunsets o'er a rose and purple sea![9]

What will you do in the life to come? Everything you were born to do. Everything you've always wanted to do. Everything the kingdom *needs* you to do.

One of the most stunning recorded moments in all history and literature took place as Jesus of Nazareth was dying on those Roman timbers.

To his right and left hung criminals, sentenced and executed for actual crimes, unlike the man between them. Those guilty men knew their hour had come. How sobering must that have been; there were no more illusions at that point, no last hope. Bitterness had already seized one convict, and he cursed his only Hope. That man was already walking on the borders of hell.

But a light was about to break into darkness for the other:

> "Jesus, remember me when you come into your
> kingdom."
> Jesus answered him, "Truly I tell you, today you
> will be with me in paradise." (Luke 23:42–43)

Have any more startling, more assuring words ever been spoken? Immensity cloistered in one dear sentence. Today. Before the sun goes down. I'm staggered by the certainty of Jesus, almost a casual certainty: "See you soon."

Remember—this is a man being tortured unto death. Yet he speaks such rock-solid promise. He must know it to be true.

CHAPTER 9

The Marriage of
Heaven and Earth

What if this present were the world's last night?

JOHN DONNE

We should talk about heaven for a moment because the new earth changes our perspective and our thoughts about our future. I want to say as clearly as I can—nothing I have written here is intended to diminish the beauty, hope, or truthfulness of heaven. Heaven is where your dear loved ones who died in Christ are now. My father is currently in heaven; so are Patrick and Craig. Should you or I die before the *palingenesia*, we will immediately be in that paradise ourselves, thank the living God. Jesus is currently in heaven too, along with our Father, the Holy Spirit, and the angels. Which makes it a breathtaking place!

> But you have come to Mount Zion, to the city of the living God, the heavenly Jerusalem. You have come to thousands upon thousands of angels in joyful assembly, to the church of the firstborn, whose names are written in heaven. You have come to God, the Judge of all, to the spirits of the righteous made perfect, to Jesus the mediator of a new covenant, and to the sprinkled blood that speaks a better word than the blood of Abel. (Hebrews 12:22–24)

Heaven is absolutely real and precious far beyond words. It is the "rest of" the kingdom of God, the "paradise" Jesus referred to. The city of God is currently there.

For the time being.

Remember—Peter explained in his sermon that Jesus remains in heaven *until* his return, when all things are made new:

> "Heaven must receive him until the time comes for God to restore everything, as he promised long ago through his holy prophets." (Acts 3:21)

Until—so much gravity and excitement contained in that word, such patient anticipation. When the time comes for God to restore everything, Jesus *leaves* heaven and comes to earth. To stay. The heavenly Jerusalem comes to earth, and

"God's dwelling place is . . . among the people" (Revelation 21:3). Heaven is not the *eternal* dwelling place of the people of God. The new earth is, just as Revelation says. Just as the entire promise of the renewal of all things says. Just as Jesus explained, and the Bible declares.

Better said, we get heaven *and* earth; both realms of God's great kingdom come together at the renewal of all things. Then will we truly say, "It's heaven on earth." For it will be.

Jesus is in heaven at this moment, but Jesus is anxiously awaiting another Day. He is readying his armies; he is cinching the straps on his saddle. There is another event his attention is absolutely fixed upon: "the Son of Man coming in his kingdom" (Matthew 16:28).

That Great and Fateful Day

Whenever the church is wrestling to understand or recover some treasure of the faith, it is always a good idea to return to what Jesus himself had to say about the matter. After all, this is his story. It is his teaching on the *palingenesia* that set us out on our wondrous journey here. Where exactly does Jesus want us to fix our future hopes?

> "Again, it will be like a man going on a journey, who called his servants and entrusted his wealth to them. . . . After a long time the master of those servants returned and settled accounts with them." (Matthew 25:14, 19)

He said: "A man of noble birth went to a distant country to have himself appointed king and then to return." (Luke 19:12)

"Therefore keep watch, because you do not know on what day your Lord will come." (Matthew 24:42)

"Be dressed ready for service and keep your lamps burning, like servants waiting for their master to return from a wedding banquet." (Luke 12:35–36)

Jesus clearly wanted us to interpret the story from the vantage point of his *return*.

Heaven is very, very precious. Heaven is the paradise of God. But if you will notice—I say this reverently, carefully—heaven is not the great anticipated event the writers of the New Testament look forward to.

And we are eagerly waiting for him to return. (Philippians 3:20 NLT)

. . . as you eagerly wait for our Lord Jesus Christ to be revealed. (1 Corinthians 1:7)

. . . looking for and hastening the coming of the day of God. (2 Peter 3:12 NKJV)

Therefore, with minds that are alert and fully sober, set your hope on the grace to be brought to you when Jesus Christ is revealed at his coming. (1 Peter 1:13)

The great hope and expectation of the Christian faith is focused on one dramatic, startling event, sudden as a bolt of lightning, sharp as the tip of a sword: the bodily return of Jesus Christ, and with that, the renewal of all things. The two are united, as surely as God the Father and God the Son are united—the renewal of all things awaits the coming of our Lord, and the coming of our Lord ushers in the renewal of all things.

Now, I know, even to mention the return of Christ suddenly gets everyone a little twitchy. There have been so many alleged "comings," and so many embarrassing disappointments (I can recall at least three in my lifetime), we just want to put this part of our faith aside and focus on other things more attractive to our age. We'd much prefer to focus on popular things like justice, the dignity of women, and God's mercy. But the historic church held the return of Christ to be so central to the Christian faith that they felt it could not be put aside or buried as some peripheral doctrine without losing Christianity itself. C. S. Lewis wrote,

There are many reasons why the modern Christian and even the modern theologian may hesitate to give to the doctrine of Christ's Second Coming that emphasis which was usually laid on it by our ancestors. Yet it seems to me impossible to retain in any recognizable form our belief in

the Divinity of Christ and the truth of the Christian revelation while abandoning, or even persistently neglecting,
the promised, and threatened, Return. "He shall come
again to judge the quick and the dead," says the Apostles'
Creed. "This same Jesus," said the angels in Acts, "shall so
come in like manner as ye have seen him go into heaven."
"Hereafter," said our Lord himself (by those words invit-
ing crucifixion), "shall ye see the Son of Man . . . coming
in the clouds of heaven." If this is not an integral part of
the faith once given to the saints, I do not know what is.[1]

Integral. Meaning critical, inextricable. Friends—the
moment you are waiting for, the event you have staked your
very life on, is the return of Christ and the renewal of all
things. Now that you understand something of the glories
of the *palingenesia*, it becomes even more the heartbeat of our
longing, our "first" and greatest hope.

But When?

Now, yes, yes—I know great damage has been done by those
who ignore the words of Christ that we cannot predict his
coming and go on to predict his coming. Announcements
were made, and the world mocked us as the predicted Day
passed without so much as a tremor. But from that fact it does
not follow that you should therefore not think about it at all.
Throughout Scripture we are urged to look for the return of

Jesus, watch for it, wait for it eagerly. And yes—it does seem that given it has been two thousand years, it could be quite a few more. But it could *also* be tonight. Our Lord and God spoke very stern warnings about a particular attitude toward his return:

> "Who then is the faithful and wise servant, whom the master has put in charge of the servants in his household to give them their food at the proper time? It will be good for that servant whose master finds him doing so when he returns. Truly I tell you, he will put him in charge of all his possessions. But suppose that servant is wicked and says to himself, 'My master is staying away a long time,' and he then begins to beat his fellow servants and to eat and drink with drunkards. The master of that servant will come on a day when he does not expect him and at an hour he is not aware of. He will cut him to pieces and assign him a place with the hypocrites, where there will be weeping and gnashing of teeth." (Matthew 24:45–51)

First, did you notice the reward again? The master puts the faithful servant in charge of *all his possessions*! He does not destroy the farm and take his servant somewhere else; he gives his servant the whole estate, the heavens and earth. But did you also notice the forbidden attitude: "my master is staying away a long time"?

Pause and let that sink in—he's "staying away a long time"

is called the "wicked" attitude. It is the *forbidden* attitude. And the one most of you probably have embraced.

> "Be dressed ready for service and keep your lamps burning, like servants waiting for their master to return from a wedding banquet, so that when he comes and knocks they can immediately open the door for him. It will be good for those servants whose master finds them watching when he comes. Truly I tell you, he will dress himself to serve, will have them recline at the table and will come and wait on them. It will be good for those servants whose master finds them ready, even if he comes in the middle of the night or toward daybreak. But understand this: If the owner of the house had known at what hour the thief was coming, he would not have let his house be broken into. You also must be ready, because the Son of Man will come at an hour when you do not expect him." (Luke 12:35–40)

We are urged to watch and be ready. Your watchfulness is further commanded with the warning that he will return at exactly the hour when everyone thinks he's still a long ways off. Like this hour right now, or any one close to it.

In order to further strengthen our hearts against the forbidden attitude, we are specifically warned about the mockers who try and diminish this hope:

> Above all, you must understand that in the last days scoffers will come, scoffing and following their own evil desires.

They will say, "Where is this 'coming' he promised? Ever since our ancestors died, everything goes on as it has since the beginning of creation." (2 Peter 3:3–4)

Where is this supposed coming? The current expression of that goes much more cleverly, like this: "But *every* age has thought that Jesus was about to show up. Even Paul did—and he was wrong. Who knows when it could be; it might take another thousand years." It sounds so reasonable . . . except for the fact that this is the forbidden attitude. Yes, every age has thought that Christ would return any moment, and well they should. They were right to do so because "any moment" could have been their moment. They were right to have expected his return because they were commanded to by Christ himself. They were wise to do so because it is the *antidote* to so many harmful things; when the "wicked servant" embraces the posture that his master is still far off, he turns his heart toward the indulgences of this world, trying to slake his kingdom thirst with everything within reach.

"At that time the kingdom of heaven will be like ten virgins who took their lamps and went out to meet the bridegroom. Five of them were foolish and five were wise. The foolish ones took their lamps but did not take any oil with them. The wise ones, however, took oil in jars along with their lamps. The bridegroom was a long time in coming, and they all became drowsy and fell asleep.

"At midnight the cry rang out: 'Here's the bridegroom! Come out to meet him!'

"Then all the virgins woke up and trimmed their lamps. The foolish ones said to the wise, 'Give us some of your oil; our lamps are going out.'

"'No,' they replied, 'there may not be enough for both us and you. Instead, go to those who sell oil and buy some for yourselves.'

"But while they were on their way to buy the oil, the bridegroom arrived. The virgins who were ready went in with him to the wedding banquet. And the door was shut.

"Later the others also came. 'Lord, Lord,' they said, 'open the door for us!'

"But he replied, 'Truly I tell you, I don't know you.'

"Therefore keep watch, because you do not know the day or the hour." (Matthew 25:1–13)

If this doesn't stir in you that good old tonic called the Fear of the Lord, I don't know what will. Half those waiting for it are "shut out" of the feast—and all that follows after. Now, I appreciate how forthright Jesus is on the matter. He admits in every story he tells that it looks like his coming is a long ways off; in this one he admits the bridegroom *was* a long time in coming(!). Jesus doesn't dodge the matter. But he goes right on with the very same lesson: keep watch; look for his coming; be ready. Keep your lamps burning, even if he comes in the second or third watch. Lewis said,

The doctrine of the Second Coming, then, is not to be rejected because it conflicts with our favorite modern mythology. It is, for that very reason, to be the more valued and made more frequently the subject of meditation. It is the medicine our condition especially needs.[2]

Meditation? We are supposed to *meditate* on his return? You have no idea what great good this does the soul until you give it a thorough try yourself. As we draw closer to the Day itself, the church begins to turn its focus from "heaven" to the coming kingdom, the restoration of all things. (The church at the end of Revelation is crying out for his return!) I guarantee you one thing, friends—we are closer now than we have ever been before. There is every reason to expect to hear that trumpet blast any day. If what this world is going through does not count as birth pangs, I honestly don't know what will.

This Changes a Lot of Things

Jesus *will* return. Swiftly, unexpectedly. Any moment. His return will usher in the renewal of all things. That includes the execution of justice, rewards, the feast, your "estates," your appointed role in his great kingdom—along with the restoration of everything you love. This has some pretty staggering implications.

For one thing, it ought to radically transform our attitude toward death.

Losing someone you love is an earthquake; it is traumatic. Because what we *see* is the death, what we *experience* is the massive sudden and ongoing loss, death is filled with tragedy and mockery. It seems to have the last word, whatever our creeds may say. We do not yet see the resurrection; we do not yet see the renewal of all things, and so we are vulnerable to massive agreements with loss and devastation, even with grief. But the moment we allow life to win, the moment we accept Jesus' "I'm just going away for a bit," it changes everything.

The day I went into the woods with the shotgun I went to face my grief head-on. After I emptied all my shells and tore up quite a few branches by hand, I collapsed on a log, my rage spent. Jesus then tenderly sidled up and asked me, *Why are you grieving?* The question felt strange, insensitive. *Why? You very well know why.* But his question had the same tone the angels used when the disciples came to the grave of Jesus on Easter morning: "Why do you look for the living among the dead?" (Luke 24:5). Jesus went on, *Craig is not dead; you know that. So let us talk about your loss.* He began to help me differentiate between grief and devastation, between "good-bye for now" and what felt like utter loss.

He asked me what difference it would make if what in fact happened was that Craig was sent to a distant land on important business. We won't hear from him for a while; he is out of cell service. But he will return, and we will share the stories of what we both have been up to. "Craig is dead" versus "Craig is gone for a while" are universes apart. He continues to exist as the person he is. He is well and about important matters. We miss him, of course, terribly; there is a hole in our lives nothing can replace. That is the loss, and it hurts. But we will see him again, so there is no place for devastation. Mourning, yes; we mourn a temporary parting.

But far too often Christians experience the death of a loved one as devastation. We even feel it is appropriate to be devastated and make massive agreements with it. By feeling utterly heartbroken we feel we are honoring the ones we have lost. But neither heaven nor the *palingenesia* leave room for devastation. Dallas Willard wrote,

> Once we have grasped our situation in God's full world, the startling disregard Jesus and the New Testament writers had for "physical death" suddenly makes sense. . . . Anyone who realizes that reality is God's, and has seen a little bit of what God has already done, will understand that such a "Paradise" would be no problem at all. And there God will preserve every one of his treasured friends in the wholeness of their personal existence precisely because he treasures them in that form. Could he enjoy their fellowship, could they serve him, if they were "dead"?[3]

I am not making light of grief nor loss. I am very familiar with them. But we must, we must keep before us the reality that our dear ones are not dead at all. They are more alive now than they have ever been. When King Caspian is "raised" from the stream a young man again, he first leaps into Aslan's arms and they exchange the strong kisses of a king and wild kisses of a lion. Caspian then turns to Eustace, with whom he sailed on his voyage to the end of the world:

> At last Caspian turned to the others. He gave a great laugh of astonished joy. "Why! Eustace!" he said. "Eustace! So you did reach the end of the world after all. What about my second-best sword that you broke on the sea-serpent?" Eustace made a step towards him with both hands held out, but then drew back with a somewhat startled expression. "Look here! I say," he stammered. "It's all very well. But aren't you?—I mean didn't you—?" "Oh, don't be such an ass," said Caspian. "But," said Eustace, looking at Aslan. "Hasn't he—er—died?" "Yes," said the Lion in a very quiet voice, almost (Jill thought) as if he were laughing. "He has died. Most people have, you know. Even I have. There are very few who haven't."[4]

Aslan is not being insensitive; he knows how awful it is to say good-bye to someone you love. He wept "great Lion-tears" for Caspian, "each tear more precious than the Earth would be if it was a single solid diamond." Jesus' own tears at the tomb of Lazarus give room for our tears too. We grieve, but our grief is utterly different from those "who have no hope," those who have not heard of the Great Restoration (1 Thessalonians 4:13).

Now, I'll be honest: I have feared my own death like most

people probably do. I have had several close calls—motorcycle accidents, mountaineering falls, some fairly hairy small plane rides—and in the moment it seemed about to happen, I feared death like any man. But after several near misses, I had to pull myself up short and ask, *What is it I am actually afraid of? What do I believe?* When I allowed my heart to speak unedited, I realized some part of me still feared total loss—the loss of everything I love. But thanks to the *palingenesia*, that fear is no longer an issue. Nothing is lost, not for the friends of God. *Nothing is lost.*

Once we allow that to be true, once we believe it in our hearts, death loses its sting, its power to intimidate.

Let me push it a step further. Jesus and the saints down through time actually *longed* for the day they left this vale of tears and stepped into Life itself. As Paul confided, "I desire to depart and be with Christ, which is better by far" (Philippians 1:23). Better by far—is that our attitude toward our own passing? It was the robust confidence and brazen boldness in the face of death that caused the early church's witness to explode across the known world. People had never seen such a thing: *Who lives like this? What secret do you know?* "We'd love to tell you."

So the desperate grasping at life you see in our world, the drastic measures when someone is well along in years, the grasp at any and every form of treatment—these should not be practiced by Christians. It makes no sense at all. Why the desperate clinging to buy yourself or a loved one a year or two more? We have lost perspective. We have forever; we have the world made new, forever. T. S. Eliot wrote a beautiful poem about the magi who visit Christ and what life was like for them when they returned to their former lives:

> We returned to our places, these Kingdoms,
> But no longer at ease here, in the old dispensation,
> With an alien people clutching their gods.
> I should be glad of another death.[5]

A sober, beautiful reminder not only of Jesus' posture toward death, but also of what we make of the false comforters in the world around us. Once we get a good look into the renewal of all things, we feel increasingly "no longer at ease here." That's not a bad thing.

THE TRUE AND ONLY HEAVEN

> Many passengers stop to take their pleasure or make their profit in the Fair, instead of going onward to the Celestial City. Indeed, such are the charms of the place that people often affirm it to be the true and only heaven; stoutly contending that there is no other, that those who seek further are mere dreamers, and that, if the fabled brightness of the Celestial City lay but a bare mile beyond the gates of Vanity, they would not be fools enough to go thither.[6]

Historian Christopher Lasch used this passage from Nathaniel Hawthorne's *The Celestial Railroad* as the premise for his book *The True and Only Heaven*, a brilliant critique on chasing any utopian dream—whether it be a social/political movement promising to address all human wrongs or our private versions to secure a "happy little life." Oh yes, you have a heart for the kingdom of God; your longing for Life is the essential part of you. And that precious heart must only be given *to* the kingdom of God, not the counterfeits so abundant in the world today. Which brings us back to shepherding our hope—and the hopes of others. Never before has the world been more in need of an unbreakable, brilliant, and tangible hope.

For the renewal of all things has a very, very sober reality to it:

I saw the Holy City, the new Jerusalem, coming down out of heaven from God, prepared as a bride beautifully dressed for her husband. And I heard a loud voice from the throne saying, "Look! God's dwelling place is now among the people, and he will dwell with them. They will be his people, and God himself will be with them and be their God. 'He will wipe every tear from their eyes. There will be no more death' or mourning or crying or pain, for the old order of things has passed away."

He who was seated on the throne said, "I am making everything new!" Then he said, "Write this down, for these words are trustworthy and true."

He said to me: "It is done. I am the Alpha and the Omega, the Beginning and the End. To the thirsty I will give water without cost from the spring of the water of life. Those who are victorious will inherit all this, and I will be their God and they will be my children. But the cowardly, the unbelieving, the vile, the murderers, the sexually immoral, those who practice magic arts, the idolaters and all liars—they will be consigned to the fiery lake of burning sulfur. This is the second death." (Revelation 21:2–8)

A shudder just ran down my spine.

Evangelism has really slipped into the background in our day, for very obvious reasons. In this climate of hatred, set in a worldwide culture of tolerance as the last remaining virtue, even the faintest suggestion that someone's opinions about faith and God might be incorrect triggers a violent reaction. The early Christians were not martyred because they believed in Jesus Christ; they were martyred because they would not *also* bow to Caesar as a god. They went to their deaths because their views were seen to be exclusivist—and indeed, they were. "Salvation is found in no one else, for there is no other name [but Jesus] under heaven given to mankind by which we must be saved" (Acts 4:12). This is the faith "once delivered"; this is your faith if you are a Christian. A very difficult line to walk at this moment.

God will make sure that everyone who wants to be there will be there. But our faith is not some soft pabulum of universal "whatever-ism." Justice cannot be justice if God were to simply ignore those who persist in hating him till the end.

Hard as it is to believe, there are many who do not *want* to be a part of God's kingdom:

> "A man of noble birth went to a distant country to have himself appointed king and then to return. So he called ten of his servants and gave them ten minas. 'Put this money to work,' he said, 'until I come back.'
>
> "But his subjects hated him and sent a delegation after him to say, 'We don't want this man to be our king.'" (Luke 19:12–14)

Startling. Inconceivable. But not everyone wants the joys of heaven-on-earth for the simple reason that they do not want Jesus to be king. His presence fills the kingdom: "The city does not need the sun or the moon to shine on it, for the glory of God gives it light" (Revelation 21:23). If you do not enjoy the highly filtered experience of his presence available now, what will you do when it is before you in fullness of glory? Theologian Gary Black gently asks,

> What is key for us to wrestle with and resolve for ourselves is whether the destiny of eternal living is something we truly desire. . . . God is the sort of person who would let into heaven anyone who . . . could possibly stand it. . . . Therefore, a great measure of what God will determine, or judge, is the degree to which any human being is prepared for the intensity of his being, and if, in the end, we would thrive or shrivel in despair and run for cover under

such weighty, glorious circumstances. As Jesus's parable of Lazarus and the rich man reveals (Luke 16), being out of God's presence was perhaps the most graceful thing God could have allowed for the rich man, given the choices he made and the person he had become.[7]

During his last time in the hospital, before he came home for hospice, Craig told me about the screaming he heard late at night in the cancer ward. "You could hear screams of terror," he said. "It wasn't pain. It was the terror of facing death alone, death without God." This is why we need to overcome our personal qualms about evangelism. My goodness—we have the most exquisite hope to offer in all the world!

When Peter warned us against the mockers, he went on to explain the reason that Jesus has not yet returned: "The Lord is not slow in keeping his promise, as some understand slowness. Instead he is patient with you, not wanting anyone to perish, but everyone to come to repentance" (2 Peter 3:9). God longs for the *palingenesia* more than anyone; but he delays and delays, in spite of human suffering, in spite of injustice, because he doesn't want anyone left out of the glorious life to come. Nor should we. These are delicate days for evangelism, but I think the wind is shifting. I think the crisis of hope sweeping the earth opens a door for us to speak to people of all cultures about our faith—especially the stunning news you now have about the restoration of all things!

Last year Stasi met a woman from India who works as a missionary there among Indian women trafficked in prostitution.

She explained to us that because of family honor these women cannot return home even if they wanted to; they are now a disgrace to the family. (Many women around the world are killed by their own families once their sexuality has been "compromised," even if it was under coercion.) Due to the rigid caste system still powerful in India, these women have no hope for another career at this point. Furthermore, the men who control them hunt down and murder any woman who attempts to leave the "trade." They have nowhere to go; these dear, beautiful women and girls have no place to turn but Jesus.

"But what do you do?" Stasi asked. "What can you offer them?" "We gather and we talk about the coming kingdom," she said. "And we worship. Their worship of Jesus is very joyful. Then they go back to their owners." Even as I report this to you, it is taking place right now; these daughters of God are living under evil every day. They have no hope but the coming kingdom. Yet they *worship*? And their worship is *joyful*? What do they know about hope that we who live in comfort are totally ignorant of? How much closer is their faith to the New Testament than mine is?

I want to know.

In my dreams last night I saw the campfires of the kingdom.

It was late into the evening; the valley before me was pitch black. I could see only the glow of scattered campfires across the hillside to my left. The setting was like you might imagine before one of the great battles of Israel or Henry V before Agincourt.

Coming closer, I saw men and angels huddled around the warmth of those fires, talking quietly. It was clearly a military operation; sentinels were posted around the camp. But the mood was confident, almost cheerful.

I saw Jesus at one of the fires, talking and laughing with his comrades. He was sharpening his arrows.

It was one of the most beautiful, encouraging pictures I've yet seen. The kingdom is on the move.

CHAPTER 10

Grab Hold with Both Hands

That's why I don't think there's any comparison between the present hard times and the coming good times. The created world itself can hardly wait for what's coming next. Everything in creation is being more or less held back. God reins it in until both creation and all the creatures are ready and can be released at the same moment into the glorious times ahead. Meanwhile, the joyful anticipation deepens.

PAUL OF TARSUS IN ROMANS 8:18–21 THE MESSAGE

There was an old wooden bridge on my grandfather's ranch; it crossed a large irrigation canal the size of a good stream, which flowed constantly with milky water the color of well-creamed coffee. Cottonwoods grew in the rich loamy soil along the canal, and their huge boughs covered it in shade all summer long. Even in the dog days of August it was always cool there, and the waters made the quietest lovely sounds as they passed under the bridge. It was a magical place for a boy. Coming in from the fields we would race the last hundred yards, galloping our horses over the bridge that boomed and echoed under our hooves with a marvelous deep sound like thunder, or cannon fire from the deck of a great ship. Swallows would shoot out from under either side, spinning away up and down the canal. As far as I was concerned, in my seven-year-old heart, that bridge had always been there and always would be. Wallace Stegner shared a similar experience from his boyhood:

> Unless everything in a man's memory of childhood is misleading, there is a time somewhere between the ages of five and twelve that corresponds to the phase ethologists have isolated in the development of birds, when an impression lasting only a few seconds may be imprinted on the young bird for life. . . . I still sometimes dream, occasionally in the most intense and brilliant shades of green, of a jungly dead bend of the Whitemud River below Martin's Dam. Each time I am haunted, on awakening, by a sense of meanings just withheld, and by a profound nostalgic melancholy. Yet why should this dead loop of river, known only for a few years, be so charged with potency in my unconscious? Why should there be around it so many other images that constantly recur in dreams or in the phrases I bring up off the typewriter onto the page? They live in me like underground water; every well I put down taps them.[1]

I now understand, some fifty years later, that the bridge under the cottonwoods was filled with "a sense of meanings" and "charged with potency" because the promise was coming to me through that place. And oh, how I would love to see it again, take my own grandchildren there; charge our horses over and make cannon fire, then sit quietly and dangle our bare feet over the edge, watching the swallows come and go. Perhaps I will, at the restoration of all things. For nothing is lost, my dear friends; *nothing is lost.*

> "I assure you that when the world is made new and the Son of Man sits upon his glorious throne . . . everyone who has given up houses or . . . property, for my sake, will receive a hundred times as much in return." (Matthew 19:28–29 NLT)

If we believed that—if we believed in the total overthrow of evil, in the complete renewal of this world, if we knew we could count on our own restoration and the exercise of our gifting in the new earth—we would be the happiest people in any world.

THE POWER OF THIS HOPE

I have been told that now, here, in the last chapter of this book, I am supposed to "make it all practical."

Several well-intentioned counselors have urged me to

finish by turning our focus to making a difference in the world today. It struck me as a hard right turn in a fast-moving train, but I've been warned that millennials especially want to talk about justice now, not heaven later. I understand the advice; I have empathy for where it comes from. But if I were you—it was spoken regarding you, dear reader—I would find it as offensive as a racial smear. As if your heart were so little and your mind so incredibly narrow you cannot possibly value the treasure of hope. As if you believe the pain of the world is due to the fact that people just have way too much hope right now.

The constant push in Western Christianity to "make it practical" betrays our favorite apostasy—it exposes how utterly fixated on the present moment we really are.

Yes, we need to embody God's love in the world today. The human race is not well; things fall apart. We must care for the planet and all creation; we must fight injustice. But we speak of that work so casually; we do not understand it can be the most demanding, heartbreaking work in the world. Those who serve at the front lines of social justice ministry have a tragically high burnout rate. Without a glorious hope blazing in your heart, you will be crushed by the pain of the world. "If you read history," wrote C. S. Lewis, "you will find that the Christians who did most for the present world were precisely those who thought most of the next. It is since Christians have largely ceased to think of the other world that they have become so ineffective in this."[2]

If you really want to make a difference in the world, the

best thing you can do is exactly what the Scriptures command you to do—grab the promised Renewal with both hands and make it the anchor of your soul:

> We who have run for our very lives to God have every reason to grab the promised hope with both hands and never let go. It's an unbreakable spiritual lifeline, reaching past all appearances right to the very presence of God. (Hebrews 6:18–19 THE MESSAGE)

People want to know: "How is God going to make it all right? How is he going to redeem all of the suffering of this world . . . and in my own life?" The answer has never been, "By this new ministry initiative!" The two thousand years since the ascension of Christ ought to make that clear. The answer has always been, "At the renewal of all things." Remember the Indian women and girls enslaved in prostitution and their joy-filled worship. As theologian Gary Black tenderly observed,

> The Bible speaks of now and forever as a continuation of a single existence. Consequently, much of the transcendent purpose God has for human life can only be properly discerned in light of eternity. Unfortunately, for an ever-increasing number of us who suffer through the pain and disillusionment of dysfunctional relationships in our families and marriages, of political or social injustice, of physical and emotional abuse, and of mental or psychological disorientation, our lives simply do not, and will

not, make sense without eternity as a backdrop on which God can manifest his endless love, redemptive power, and enabling grace. Such a perspective alone has the potential to revolutionize the universe.[3]

If you woke each morning and your heart leapt with hope, knowing that the renewal of all things was just around the corner—might even come today—you would be one happy person. If you knew in every fiber of your being that nothing is lost, that everything will be restored to you and then some, you would be armored against discouragement and despair. If your heart's imagination were filled with rich expectations of all the goodness coming to you, your confidence would be contagious; you would be unstoppable, revolutionary.

Friends—don't you let anyone or anything cheat you of this hope; it is your spiritual lifeline. You have barely begun to take hold of it. Do not let anything diminish the beauty, power, and significance of this hope above all hopes. Jesus lived the way he did in this world, *for* this world, because his hope was set *beyond* this world; that is the secret of his life. "Study how he did it. Because he never lost sight of where he was headed—that exhilarating finish in and with God—he could put up with anything along the way: Cross, shame, whatever. And now he's there, in the place of honor, right alongside God" (Hebrews 12:2 THE MESSAGE).

Oh yes, we need to make this practical. We need to take this hope so seriously we sell everything to buy this field. We must make this utterly real and tangible, so that over time our souls are truly anchored by it. Of all things we could do that would be the most practical, that has the most staggering implications.

GIVING OUR HEARTS TO THE KINGDOM

Here is a good beginning—what are the first three things you plan to do when you enter the kingdom?

I'm serious. What are the first three things you plan to do at the renewal of all things? You should begin making lists, allow yourself to dream, and dream big. For the simple reason that if this is not something you are making plans for, then your hopes are not really set there.

What are the first three things you want to do? Where are the first three places you want to visit? Is there some special spot like my old bridge from your childhood that you would love to return to? The sound of the rain on a tin roof as you fell asleep at night? The smell of orange sticky buns fresh from the oven on Christmas morning? Remember—it is the child-heart in you that is far readier to embrace the kingdom. This isn't wishful thinking; this isn't "How enchanting!" Either you believe the kingdom is coming, or you do not. If you do believe, now you understand that the kingdom means the restoration of all things: "Look, I am making everything new!" (Revelation 21:5 NLT).

Given the suffocating, pathological unbelief and anti-romanticism of our post-postmodern culture, you are going to have to make very conscious choices to take hold of this hope. Allowance—*the renewal of all things might be true*—is not taking hold. Acceptance—*okay, I think it is*—is not taking hold. We need to grab this hope like we would hug the person in front of us if we were passengers on a wild motorcycle ride; we need to "take hold" like you do the top of a ladder when you suddenly think you are falling. *Seize* is a far better description; we need to *seize* this hope.

It might help you to ask again—like we did in chapter 1—*How is my hope these days? Where is my hope these days?* To shepherd your first hope for the treasure it is, you need to be aware of what you are currently doing with hope right now. Have you attached precious hopes to causal things, your first hope to just about anything?

Several years ago I had a dream come true, a lifelong dream to bow hunt moose in the wilds of the Yukon. We were as remote in the wilderness as I've ever been. After our floatplane dropped us off to make the farther trek into the Jennings River valley, our guide told us the wildlife we encountered would probably never have seen a human being. Wolves. Grizzly bears. Moose so large they stand eight feet at the *shoulder*. It was a breathtaking experience, and I had *so much* hope set on it. It was the trip of a lifetime. But like so many things in this life, the reality fell short of my expectations. The weather wasn't good; we didn't sleep well; the moose weren't around.

As those precious I-will-never-do-this-again-in-my-life days ticked by, the emotional roller coaster was miserable:

hope and despair, hope and despair, every day. Hiking back to camp the night of day six, cold and dejected, I finally prayed, *Jesus, you've got to catch my heart.* Suddenly this verse from 1 Peter came to my heart: "Set your hope on the grace to be brought to you when Jesus Christ is revealed" (1:13). It was not what I wanted to hear; I wanted to hear, *Your moose is coming!* But Jesus knew exactly what I needed. Set my hope *fully* on his return? I don't think at the moment my hopes were even set partially there. Not in practicality; not in day-to-day living. I believe in the kingdom; I believe everything I have written here. But I keep giving my kingdom heart to things like that dream trip; I keep putting my ultimate hopes in places they shouldn't be.

By way of contrast, let me tell you a recent story about my daughter-in-law—the one who lost her dear brother. Emilie and Blaine are wilderness souls; I think if they could live in a tepee, they would. This summer, the summer of heartache, they planned to use their vacation time for a backpacking trip with close friends from out of state. The rendezvous point was the Wind River Mountains in Wyoming—some of the last real wilderness left in the lower forty-eight. But a little complication came along: Em was seven months pregnant. Canceling seemed the right thing to do. Emilie said, "Never mind. I'll see them at the Restoration."

The effect was so startling and refreshing, it was nearly magical—as if she had thrown back the curtains and flung the windows open in a darkened house shut up for years. Startling, because, well—have *you* ever heard anyone take the restoration of all things for granted in such an assured way? She said it so matter-of-factly: "I'll see them at the Restoration." Refreshing because, well—it was like hearing the perspective of those who live in the kingdom of God right now. Who here lives with this perspective? But this is THE perspective, the one true perspective, the perspective of Jesus and his very close friends down through the centuries. It is meant to be our daily perspective. As opposed to, say, all those "fifty places you need to fish/surf/golf/dine at/see before you die" books.

So another way to begin to seize this hope with a good, firm grip is to ask yourself, *What have I done with my kingdom heart? Where am I currently taking it?* You have a heart for joy— where is your hope for joy set right now? You have a heart for redemption—where are you taking your heart for redemption these days? You ache for restoration, yours and those you love—where is your hope for restoration these days?

What I am suggesting is that we need to begin to make conscious, deliberate decisions to give our hearts to the return of Jesus and the renewal of all things. Every time you find yourself getting anxious about an uncertain hope, stop and pray, *Jesus, I give my hope to your true and certain return, and the renewal of all things.* Every time disappointment strikes again, you pray, *Jesus, I give my heart to your kingdom; I am made for your kingdom and nothing else will do.* When you wake in the morning and all your hopes and fears rush at you; when you come home at night beat up from another long day and all you want to do is medicate; when you hear of someone else's great joy and something envious rises in you—make the conscious decision to give your heart to the return of Christ and the restoration of all things.

And especially when you experience loss. Oh, friends—can we remember that life is a long series of good-byes? You have suffered so many losses already; we hate to admit it, but many more are yet to come. But now we can say to ourselves, *Nothing is truly lost. This is going to come back to me; this will be in one of my treasure chests Jesus will restore to me.*

Friends, it is as simple as this: if you do not give your heart over to the renewal of all things, you *will* take your kingdom heart to something in this world. You will do compulsive things, like collecting way too many shoes. You will be tempted into far darker things. It is inevitable.

But if you will begin to choose the kingdom—"seek ye first" (Matthew 6:33 KJV)—if you consciously and deliberately give your heart to the renewal of all things, you will notice the effects immediately. So much pressure will be lifted off your current hopes; when things don't go well, you'll find yourself less angry, less dejected. As your heart and soul become anchored in the Renewal, you'll find yourself freer to risk, especially love. You can love people, because God will do everything in his power to make sure you will not lose them; the good-byes of his children are only momentary. You can love beautiful places and cultures and things like wilderness because even though it looks like they may be vanishing, they will be restored.

For nothing is lost. He renews all things.

Filling the Treasury of
Your Imagination

The dreams I began having about the kingdom only started this year. I have friends who seem to "see into" the kingdom, but I have never been that guy. I do hear from God; his words to me are precious beyond telling. But I've never been one to receive "pictures" or visions, let alone dreams. Then one day it struck me: *Maybe the reason I don't get pictures from God is because I don't ask for them.* "You do not have because you do not ask" (James 4:2). So I began asking.

And God began answering. Not only in dreams, but in all sorts of ways (he is eager to fill our hearts with hope!).

The sunrise out my window has become a regular reminder for me; I've come to look for the promise there every morning. I keep running into images of the kingdom in photos I see, so I've started to cut pictures out of magazines; I want to build a scrapbook of images of the new earth. In fact, I spent several hours online last week looking through one of those stock photo websites, looking for images that had the special magic for me of the Great Renewal.

Movies are also filled with pictures of the Restoration. Stasi and I were watching *Tangled*—the Disney story of a princess stolen by an evil woman and held captive for decades. Every year her father and mother—the king and queen— release lanterns into the sky to commemorate her birthday and to proclaim the hope she will return one day. Far off in her prison tower, the captive princess sees those lanterns and something in her heart knows they are for her. Finally, she breaks free of the witch and makes it back to the city in time to see those lanterns for herself. A silly moment for the kingdom to break through, but I found myself quietly weeping for the day I get to come home to my Father-King, and the reception he will have for me.

You will be greatly helped by filling the treasury of your imagination with images of the coming Renewal; without them, it will be nigh impossible to make this the anchor of your soul. If you would take hold of this hope with both hands and never let go, you need to know what it is you are taking hold of. "I Can Only Imagine" became a hit song about heaven, but that's just the problem—when we say to ourselves, "I can only imagine," what we really mean is, "I *can't* imagine how wonderful it will be," and since you can't imagine it, you can't hope for it. The foggy and vague do not inspire, ever. As Peter Kreeft says, "It doesn't matter whether it's a dull lie or a dull truth. Dullness, not doubt, is the strongest enemy of faith."[4]

Ask Jesus to show you his kingdom.

Sanctify your imagination to him, all your spiritual gifting, and ask him to reveal to you pictures of the coming kingdom. Be specific—if you want to see the city, ask to see the city. If you want to see those waterfalls, ask to see them. You will need to be open to being surprised; do not "script" what you think you "should" see. I dreamed of ships last night—great, three-masted sailing ships. The day was clear and bright, and we were tacking into the trade winds, driving our prow through the surf at a wonderful speed. I saw other ships to my right and left, and I realized we were racing. The ocean was aquamarine, clearer than usual; I could see marine life below us, keeping pace with us. It helped to shatter my lingering religious fears that heaven is going to be boring!

Stay open to surprises; keep asking for glimpses of the kingdom any way God wants to bring them. This is how we reach into the future to take hold of the hope that is our anchor. The more our imaginations seize upon the reality, the more we will have confident expectation of all the goodness coming to us.

And if you want to take a really big risk, for an even more beautiful and encouraging picture, ask Jesus to show you as he sees you, as you are in his kingdom. That one might take a little waiting for, because we are so fearful, but wait for it. It will be worth it.

Welcoming the Promise in a New Way

We have been looking for the kingdom all our lives. When we were children, we searched for it in ponds and corn-fields, attics and bedroom forts we'd make with blankets. We "found" it in fairy tales and our favorite stories. All your life you have been looking for this kingdom. You'll hear a certain song or piece of music, and it brings you to tears because it is haunting you with the kingdom. All your special places or those you dream of going—the longing you have for them is

not because the kingdom is there, but rather because it is calling to you through that place, the aromas, the way you feel
when you are there.

God knew he had to woo our hearts forward into the
Restoration, so he wove the promise of it into the earth.
Now you understand why that promise fits perfectly with a
wild hope deep within our hearts, a hope we hardly dare to
name. As we live forward from here, we can now interpret
the promise rightly; we can embrace it for we know what it is.
These glimpses can help fill the treasury of our imagination.

Fall has nearly passed now in the high country; we had
our first snow last night. I have been savoring every beautiful day. Does it seem strange that as I walk in the evenings
I pause at every last wildflower, treasuring it as much as I
do in spring when the first flowers arrive? Last night after
dinner I was walking through the woods behind our home,
touching the water-colored leaves, holding them in my hands
lovingly, saying, "Thank you for coming. I'll miss you. Please
come back."

The aspens in our yard are a lovely golden hue; at least
those with leaves are. Most have shed them all. With apologies
to Robert Frost, I want to point out that nature's *last* green is
also gold. The leaves were trembling in a slight breeze yesterday evening. Trembling in anticipation. It's as if nature knows
a great secret and can hardly keep it in. Fall is like a sunset,
and it whispers the secret of the sunset if we have ears to hear.
I stand among aspen leaves the color of the streets of the city
of God, listening to creation whisper, *This loss heralds a great*

return. Something golden is just around the corner. But you must let this go in order to find that.

LIVING EXPECTANTLY

The renewal of all things is the most beautiful, hopeful, glorious promise ever made in any story, religion, philosophy, or fairy tale.

And it is *real*.

And it is *yours*.

As you begin to see for yourself, you will find hoping in it rather easy, and as you place your hopes in it you will be the most grounded person you know. So allow me, before we close, to turn your heart there one last time: What are the first three things you plan to do at the renewal of all things? I'll share mine, to help you begin to name yours:

I'm going to run and jump into the arms of Jesus. (Oh, friends, we will finally be with Jesus.) He and I will throw our heads back and laugh—the laughter of good friends reunited, the laughter of victors who have overcome. We will savor the laughter of kindred spirits who share in the greatest of all triumphs—that it was all true, that life can now begin.

Then I'm going to the feast to search for dear ones I have lost. Though I'm sure I won't have to look very far; I know in his kindness our Host will have seated us at tables close together. I'll swap jokes with Craig, just like old times. I'll hug Patrick for the first time. I will welcome my own children back from having to say good-bye to me in this life. We, too, will laugh, surprised at how much more wonderful it all is than we dreamed, and yet how very like we thought it would be too.

And afterward, after that long and glorious celebration where every story is told rightly and rewards are lavishly given, I am going to find the stables of the city, find those horses that have played a part in our story here. Together with my family I will ride through the gates and out into open country, riding like the wind through the fields of tall grasses as the King's horses come and run with us. For all creation will be ours again, and like the child-hearted we will be, play shall be the first order of business. Perhaps in our adventures we will come across a bridge under great cottonwoods. We will charge our horses over and make cannon fire, then sit quietly and dangle our bare feet over the edge, watching the swallows come and go—relishing the freshness of all things made new.

Acknowledgments

This book simply would not have been possible without the brilliant research skills of my son Luke Eldredge, nor the mighty prayers offered by the men and women who prayed for me through the writing process. My thanks as well to my publisher, Brian Hampton; my editor, Webster Younce; and the teams at Nelson and Yates and Yates. We will toast this one at the feast.

About the Author

John Eldredge is the author of many popular works, including *Wild at Heart*, *Captivating* (with his wife, Stasi), *Beautiful Outlaw*, and a dozen other titles. He is founder and director of Ransomed Heart—a discipleship ministry based in Colorado. John earned his master's degree in counseling from Colorado Christian University, but he spends most of his free time in the outdoors chasing wildlife and various adventures. You can find details about John's podcast and live events on his website, www.ransomedheart.com.

Notes

Introduction

1. National Center for Health Statistics, "Health, United States, 2010: With Special Feature on Death and Dying," Table 95, https://www.cdc.gov/nchs/data/hus/hus10.pdf.
2. World Health Organization, "Depression: Fact Sheet," April 2016, http://www.who.int/mediacentre/factsheets/fs369/en/.
3. Sabrina Tavernise, "U.S. Suicide Rate Surges to a 30-Year High," *New York Times*, April 21, 2016, https://www.nytimes.com/2016/04/22/health/us-suicide-rate-surges-to-a-30-year-high.html?_r=0; Centers for Disease Control and Prevention (CDC), Web-Based Injury Statistics Query and Reporting System (WISQARS), 2013, 2011, National Center for Injury Prevention and Control, CDC, https://www.cdc.gov/violenceprevention/suicide/statistics/index.html; Gregg Zoroya, "Suicide Surpassed War as the Military's Leading Cause of Death," *USA Today*, October 31, 2014, http://www.usatoday.com/story/nation/2014/10/31/suicide-deaths-us-military-war-study/18261185/.

Chapter 1: Is There a Hope That Really Overcomes All This?

1. "Outlandish Proverbs", ed. George Herbert, in *The Complete Works in Verse and Prose of George Herbert*, vol. 3 (1640; repr., London: Robson and Sons, 1874), 324.

2. Lilas Trotter, quoted in *Many Beautiful Things*, directed by Laura Waters Hinson (Oxvision Films LLC, 2015).

3. Matthew 6:34.

4. Victoria Woollaston, "How Often Do You Check Your Phone?" dailymail.com, October 29, 2015, http://www.dailymail.co.uk/sciencetech/article-3294994/How-check-phone-Average-user-picks-device-85-times-day-twice-realise.html.

5. Alexia LaFata, "Texting Has the Same Effect as an Orgasm, That's Why You're Addicted," *Elite Daily*, November 12, 2014, http://elitedaily.com/life/culture/receiving-text-message-like-orgasm/845037/.

6. "Illegal Drug Use," Centers for Disease Control and Prevention, April 27, 2016, http://apps.who.int/medicinedocs/documents/s19032en/s19032en.pdf.

7. Katie Rogers, "Leslie Jones, Star of 'Ghostbusters,' Becomes a Target of Online Trolls," *New York Times*, July 19, 2016, http://www.nytimes.com/2016/07/20/movies/leslie-jones-star-of-ghostbusters-becomes-a-target-of-online-trolls.html?_r=0.

8. Jerome Groopman, *The Anatomy of Hope: How People Prevail in the Face of Illness* (New York: Random House, 2005), xvi; Stacy Lu, "Turning Lives Around with Hope," *American Psychological Association* 45, no. 10 (2014): 26; Caroline Leaf, *Switch On Your Brain* (Grand Rapids: Baker, 2013), 31–53.

9. Dante, *Inferno*, Canto III, (Edinburgh, UK: Edinburgh University Press, 1884). Kindle edition.

10. G. K. Chesterton, *William Blake* (London: Duckworth; New York: Dutton, 1910), 131.

11. "Imelda Marcos," *Wikipedia*, accessed May 17, 2016, https://en.wikipedia.org/wiki/Imelda_Marcos.

12. C. S. Lewis, *The Problem of Pain* (New York: Macmillan, 1945), 134.

CHAPTER 2: THE RENEWAL OF ALL THINGS

1. Blaise Pascal, *Pensées* (London: HarperCollins, 1995), 63.
2. Dallas Willard, *The Divine Conspiracy* (San Francisco: HarperCollins, 1998), 395.
3. N. T. Wright, *Surprised by Hope* (New York: HarperOne, 2008), 93.
4. P. G. Müller, *Exegetical Dictionary of the New Testament*, vol. 1, ed. Horst Balz and Gerhard Schneider (1978; repr., Grand Rapids, MI: Eerdmans), 129–30.
5. Wright, *Surprised by Hope*, 104.
6. Eva K. Neumaier-Dargyay, "Buddhism," in *Life after Death in World Religions*, ed. Harold Coward (Maryknoll, NY: Orbis Books, 1997), 87–93; Axel Michaels, *Hinduism: Past and Present* (Princeton: Princeton University Press, 2004), 154–58.
7. C. S. Lewis, *Essay Collections and Other Short Pieces* (New York: HarperCollins, 2000), 9.

CHAPTER 3: LET US BE HONEST

1. Charles Dickens, *A Christmas Carol* (1843; repr., Mineola, NY: Dover, 1991), 61.
2. Nathaniel Hawthorne, "The Old Manse," in *Mosses from an Old Manse*, vol. 1 (1846; repr., New York: Modern Library, 2003), 21–22.
3. "Assassin's Creed," Wikipedia, accessed January 30, 2017, https://en.wikipedia.org/wiki/Assassin%27s_Creed; "The Elder Scrolls," Wikipedia, accessed January 30, 2017, https://en.wikipedia.org/wiki/The_Elder_Scrolls.
4. "Global Report on Trafficking in Persons 2014," UNODC

(United Nations Office on Drugs and Crime), United Nations
Sales No. E.14.V.10, http://www.unodc.org/documents/
data-and-analysis/glotip/GLOTIP_2014_full_report.pdf;
"Pornography Statistics: Annual Report 2015," Covenant Eyes,
http://www.covenanteyes.com/pornstats/; "Adverse Childhood
Experiences Study: Data and Statistics"; CDC: Injury Prevention
and Control, http://www.cdc.gov/nccdphp/ace/prevalence.htm.

5. Henri Nouwen, *Out of Solitude: Three Meditations on Christian Life* (Notre Dame, IN: Ave Maria Press, 2004), 53.

6. Blaise Pascal, *Pensées* (Indianapolis: Hacket, 2004), 219.

CHAPTER 4: THE NEW EARTH

1. J. R. R. Tolkien, *The Lord of the Rings* (1954; repr., New York: Houghton Mifflin Harcourt, 2004), 281.

2. G. K. Chesterton, *Orthodoxy* (1908; repr., Chicago: Moody Classics, 2009), 20–22.

3. Ibid., 82.

4. Tolkien, *Lord of the Rings*, 35–41.

5. John Muir, "The Yosemite National Park," *Atlantic Monthly* (1899) 2002, http://www.theatlantic.com/past/docs/issues/1899aug/muir.htm.

6. Jess Zimmerman, "Elephants Hold Vigil for Human Friend," Grist, May 14 2012, http://grist.org/animals/elephants-hold-vigil-for-human-friend/.

7. "How Many Words Do Dogs Know?" Animal Planet, accessed January 30, 2017, http://www.animalplanet.com/pets/how-many-words-do-dogs-know; A. Andics, A. Gábor, M. Gácsi, T. Faragó, D. Szabó, and Á. Miklósi, "Neural Mechanisms for Lexical Processing in Dogs," *Science* 353.6303 (2016): 1030–32. DOI: 10.1126/science.aaf3777.

8. "Dolphin Communication," Dolphin Research Center, accessed January 30, 2017, https://www.dolphins.org/communication.

9. Nick Jans, *A Wolf Called Romeo* (Boston: Houghton, Mifflin Harcourt, 2014).

10. George MacDonald, quoted in Rolland Hein, ed., *The Heart of George MacDonald* (Wheaton, IL: Harold Shaw, 1994), 15.

11. C. S. Lewis, *God in the Dock* (Grand Rapids: Eerdmans, 1970), 87, emphasis mine.

12. C. S. Lewis, *The Last Battle* (New York: HarperCollins, 2002), 213–14, 219.

CHAPTER 5: OUR RESTORATION

1. C. S. Lewis, *The Silver Chair* (New York: HarperCollins, 1953), 237–39.

2. George Herbert, *Herbert: Poems* (London: Random House, 2004), 215.

3. See chapter 1 in my book *Beautiful Outlaw* (New York: FaithWords, 2011).

4. 2 Samuel 6:12–15.

5. Psalm 103:12.

6. Bessel van der Kolk, *The Body Keeps the Score* (New York: Penguin, 2014), 280, 282.

7. Gary Black, *Preparing for Heaven* (New York: HarperOne, 2015), 29.

8. Stanley Kunitz, *The Collected Poems of Stanley Kunitz* (1978; repr., New York: W. W. Norton, 2002), 217.

9. C. S. Lewis, *The Horse and His Boy* (New York: HarperCollins, 1954), 221–22.

10. Richard Louv, *Last Child in the Woods* (Chapel Hill, NC: Algonquin Books, 2005), overall theme of the book.

CHAPTER 6: WHEN EVERY STORY IS TOLD RIGHTLY

1. C. S. Lewis, *On Stories and Other Essays on Literature* (New York: Harcourt, 1966), 83.

2. 1 Corinthians 16:13 NASB.
3. Thomas Cahill points this out in *How the Irish Saved Civilization* (New York: Random House, 1995).
4. *Beowulf*, trans. Seamus Heaney (New York: W. W. Norton, 2000), 13.
5. Ibid., 15.
6. Ibid., 45.
7. Ibid., 69.
8. Ibid., 69–70.
9. Ibid., 97.
10. Cahill, *How the Irish Saved Civilization*, 117–18.
11. C. S. Lewis, *The Weight of Glory* (New York: Touchstone, 1975), 26.
12. C. S. Lewis, *The Voyage of the Dawn Treader* (New York: Collier, 1952), 96–97.
13. Ibid., 100.
14. C. S. Lewis, *The Silver Chair*, (New York: HarperCollins, 1953), 21.
15. J. R. R. Tolkien, *The Lord of the Rings*, (1954; repr., New York: Houghton Mifflin Harcourt, 2004), 952–53.

CHAPTER 7: THE OVERTHROW OF EVIL

1. John Milton, *Paradise Lost* (1667; repr., New York: W. W. Norton, 2004), 28–29.
2. C. S. Lewis, *The Lion, the Witch and the Wardrobe* (1950; repr., New York: Harper, 1978), 142.
3. Ibid., 161–62.
4. J. R. R. Tolkien, *The Lord of the Rings,* (1954; repr., New York: Houghton Mifflin Harcourt), 842.
5. "Prostitution Statistics," Havocscope: Global Black Market Information, http://www.havocscope.com /prostitution-statistics.

CHAPTER 8: WHAT DO WE ACTUALLY DO?

1. Dallas Willard, *The Divine Conspiracy* (San Francisco: HarperCollins, 1998), 399.
2. Ibid., 378.
3. Jean Giono, *The Man Who Planted Trees* (London: Peter Owen, 1989), 8.
4. Ibid., 17–18.
5. Ibid., 23–25.
6. Ibid., 34, 37–38.
7. Ibid., 39.
8. N. T. Wright, quoted in David Van Biema, "Christians Wrong About Heaven, Says Bishop," *Time*, February 7, 2008, http://content.time.com/time/world/article/0,8599,1710844,00.html.
9. George MacDonald, *Diary of an Old Soul* (Minneapolis: Augsburg, 1994), 30.

CHAPTER 9: THE MARRIAGE OF HEAVEN AND EARTH

1. C. S. Lewis, *The World's Last Night and Other Essays* (New York: Harcourt, 1952), 93.
2. Ibid., 106.
3. Dallas Willard, *The Divine Conspiracy* (San Francisco: HarperCollins, 1998), 84–85.
4. C. S. Lewis, *The Silver Chair*, (New York: HarperCollins, 1953), 239.
5. T. S. Eliot, *Collected Poems 1909–1962* (San Diego, CA: Harcourt Brace Jovanovich, 1963), 99–100.
6. Nathaniel Hawthorne, *Hawthorne's Short Stories* (1946; repr., New York: Vintage, 1973), 243.
7. Black, *Preparing for Heaven*, 91, 127–28.

CHAPTER 10: GRAB HOLD WITH BOTH HANDS

1. Wallace Stegner, *Marking the Sparrow's Fall* (New York: Henry Holt and Company, 1992), 5–6.

2. C. S. Lewis, *Mere Christianity* (1952; New York: HarperOne, 1980), 135.

3. Gary Black, *Preparing for Heaven*, (New York: HarperOne, 2015), 38.

4. Peter Kreeft, *Everything You Ever Wanted to Know About Heaven* (San Francisco: Ignatius Press, 1990), 20.

DEFIANT JOY

by STASI ELDREDGE

Introduction

Why *Defiant Joy*? Why not read a book simply on joy? The answer is an easy one. In this world where we find ourselves living, having joy often feels both crazy and out of reach. That's why the title of this book includes the word *defiant*. Defiant means to stand against the tide. It means to go against the flow, even when the flow is composed of a strong current of despair and difficulty.

To have joy in the midst of sorrow—or the current news feed—can seem impossible. And all on our own, it is impossible. But just as the angel Gabriel said after making his outlandish proclamation to Mary that she, a virgin, would give birth to the Savior of the world, "Nothing will be impossible with God" (Luke 1:37 NASB).

Joy is meant to be ours, a joy that is defiant in the face of this broken world. Our hearts are to echo the heartbeat

---

of our joyous God. Now, this isn't about skipping around in the garden singing, "I'm so happy in Jesus every day." This is about being present to whatever may be coming our way and, in the midst of both the goodness and the grief, knowing joy.

Believing that sorrow and loss do not have the final word takes defiance. It requires a strength of spirit that must be nurtured. It means engaging our lives fully but interpreting them by the highlight of heaven. Denying the truth of reality is not the answer; being fully present to it is.

The invitation from God to "rejoice, again I say rejoice" comes to us in the middle of our lowest lows as well as our highest highs. How do we do that? Let's find out together.

CHAPTER 1

A Holy Defiance

Joy is the serious business of Heaven.
—C. S. Lewis

It is a quiet morning. The house is empty save for our two resigned dogs—resigned because they sense this master will not be taking them on a walk anytime soon. They know it from my slow movements, which cause their natural exuberance to dim. This morning, I will not allow myself to be baited by their soft, desire-filled eyes. *Sorry, guys. The bed is just too cozy, and it's my day off.*

Suddenly the quiet is broken as my youngest golden, Maisie, still a puppy by every standard, dashes from my bedside and begins to bark indignantly. I can guess the reason. It is the bark she uses to alert all within earshot that some neighboring cow has trespassed onto her property. Looking out my bedroom window, I see a confused little black bovine, backside still raw with the telltale signs of a too-new brand, wandering along our side of the fence. Our offended dog will let this calf, separated from her lumbering mother, know her mistake. There will be no reunions on Maisie's front porch.

In the peace that returns after Maisie calms down, having barked the calf on her way, I notice the air smells of smoke. It is the height of summer now: fire season. There is a fire burning somewhere close. Too close.

The smell of smoke used to be one I liked. It is reminiscent of campfires and conversations, marshmallows when I was young. Now, though, I am too closely acquainted with forest fires. We've lived through three fires since moving to Colorado, but the Waldo Canyon fire that swept through Colorado in 2012, burning 347 homes and swallowing 18,000 acres of gorgeous forest, had come the closest. The hungry flames came within twenty feet of our house. The courageous firefighters and Vandenberg Air Force Base "Hot Shots" gave it up for lost, taking their stand across our street against the raging inferno. We evacuated in speed, shock, and tears, and for long minutes we did not know if we would live or die, swallowed up by flames ourselves. No. I no longer find the fragrance of smoke comforting.

Flames are licking all around us, aren't they? All the time. Saint Peter describes our life here on this earth as a "fiery ordeal" (1 Peter 4:12). Tragedies and heartache and pressures and illnesses and irritations grand and small show up

indiscriminately, and they do not limit themselves to one season. I become very sick, but my husband becomes much more
ill at the same time—and my children hit a crisis and the call
comes telling us of a loved one dying and the letter arrives
from the IRS telling us we are going to be audited and the
plea for help arrives in our inbox from a friend because her
son is suicidal and the deadline for a project is pending and
another friend has found a lump in her breast, and all this
occurs within two days.

Life is hard, and it doesn't seem to let up.

I know that in comparison to most, my own life has not
been so bad. I am not a refugee. I am not living in the middle
of a drought-filled land, praying that my child will survive
another day. My daily reality is not set in a war zone (well, at
least not one that can be seen). I am not living on the streets.
I have a roof over my head. I have running water that will
not make me ill. When I put my feet on the floor after a
night's sleep, there is carpet underneath them. I am a resident
of the United States and living a life of luxury in comparison
to 90 percent of the human population. I'm very aware of
all this.

But such facts, though true and humbling, don't help me
most of the time. Too often they serve only to shame me
and keep me from being present to the sorrow in my life
that threatens to swallow up everything, like a forest fire that
looms near. Too near. Yes, I want to be aware of others in
the world. I do want to grow in compassion, but that will
require me to feel my own pain, to not run from it through

comparisons that only serve to diminish my own hard. When I do not have compassion for myself in my own trials, my compassion for others also goes down—both for those whose sorrows I have known in part and those whose sorrows I have not. Besides, the grace of God is not present in my comparisons. It is here for me in my moment. If I run from my reality, I also run from the presence of God.

So my heart scans the horizon in the quiet of the morning when the faint smell of smoke rises, and I ask, "Where are You, God?"

And the answer comes from deep within. "I'm right here."

DEFIANCE, NOT DENIAL

Our home had been overtaken by fairy lights. Christmas twinkle lights, boughs of evergreens, ribbons of red, and the fragrance of pine filled the living room. It was the night of our annual Christmas party, and I was ready. I'd been decorating for weeks. Even the bathroom had a little sleigh in it.

Once a year our team gathers in our home to celebrate all that God has done through our little ministry. We reflect. We give thanks. We feast. We laugh. And we get all dressed up to do it. Plus, it's catered, so there's that. It's planned two months in advance, and as it draws near the expectation of joy rises exponentially.

That year, I had a spare moment on the afternoon of the party before I needed to get dressed, so, as is often the case, I went online to check out what was happening in the world. Take a look at emails. Update my Facebook status.

When I did, I learned what had transpired that day and wept with shock and despair. My soul was filled with anger and deep sorrow.

A lone gunman had opened fire on elementary school–aged children, killing twenty six- and seven-year-olds in a terrifying and horrific spree. Six adult staff were also shot and killed. It was the deadliest shooting at any school in the United States. After brutally taking these precious lives, the gunman had committed suicide.

I found my husband and told him of the tragedy. We wept and prayed together. Then, as we thought about all the people who were about to show up at our house, we wondered, *How could we celebrate life in the face of such wickedness and loss?*

And that's when the phrase "defiant joy" was born. We would not cancel the party. We would gather. We would not pretend that the shootings had not taken place, nor would we forget that a whole community was grieving the children lost, but we would proclaim that even so, *even so*, there was a reason to celebrate—particularly since it was Christmastime, when we gather to honor and remember the invasion of the kingdom of God. That's what Christmas is, you know. It's an *invasion*.

The battle between good and evil could not have been made starker on that day, and it looked like a victory for the kingdom of darkness. But we needed to remember that Jesus had entered the darkness and brought the light. His unending life signaled the end to the rule of evil and proclaimed the ultimate victory of the kingdom of God. Yes, a battle was raging, but Jesus had won it, and we were invited to proclaim it and enforce it.

Once everyone had gathered in our home that night, we paused and prayed and, in silence, honored the lives lost and the families forever changed. And then we turned our hearts to the One who is our hope in the face of loss and untold grief. Because of Jesus—His death, His resurrection, and His ascension—we chose to honor Him and celebrate that He has won and is winning still.

We feasted. We talked long into the night by candlelight and Christmas music. We lingered in one another's presence, drawing closer to the fire of each other's hearts than we might otherwise have done *because* of the pain. We were defiantly joyful.

Defiant joy is different from mere defiance. And it is completely other than denial.

———— ✺ ————

April 26, 2001, 11:00 a.m. My mother had just died. Her passing was a holy one. My sisters, aunt, and I were gathered around her bed in her home, singing her into eternity. It was a precious and sacred time, made even more so by our sharing it together. At 1:00 p.m., the somber, respectful men in their dark suits came with a stretcher to take her body away. It was at this moment that the reality of our loss hit one of my sisters and hit her hard. She needed more time with my mother. Years of being physically and emotion-ally distant caught up with her. Now she refused to let the chagrined men do their work. They eventually had to leave empty-handed.

That turned out to be okay, though, because it allowed time for my aunt to take pictures. It must be a North Dakota thing. An old-world thing. I don't know. It's not my thing. My aunt carefully placed flowers around my mother's lovely departed self and snapped away. When forty-five photos of my dead mother arrived a month later, I wasn't quite sure what I was supposed to do with them. Frame one?

Hours after the terrified funeral workers left, they returned, stretcher again in hand. My sister would have none of it. The rest of us thought we might have to resort to drugs. Or a straitjacket. Whether those devices would be for her or for us, we weren't sure.

A body without the spirit does not linger well. My moth-er's body needed to be lent into the care of others. Fortunately my brother was in the house. Strong. Firm. Determined. And angry. He had chosen not to view my mother's body after she had passed on to her forever home, but my sister's pain forced him to. He had to go into my mother's bedroom and convince my sister to let her go.

It was with sorrow, with unabsorbed grief, and with a camera snapping that I stood by as they finally wheeled my mother's body past.

What is one to do after such a moment but acquiesce to my aunt's offer to go get some dinner?

Okay. You betcha. Super. Besides, she had already chosen the restaurant.

In shell shock, we all piled into her car as she drove us to a teppanyaki restaurant. Do you know the kind I'm talking about? It's the one where diners gather around a common table while the chef awes the guests with his prowess with cutlery. Up in the air goes the zucchini. Down come the chopped spirals. I had no words.

There we were, reeling from the trauma not only of my mother's passing but from my sister's heart-wrenching grief, and we were supposed to be cheering for an onion volcano. Suffice it to say, we were not the chef's best audience that night.

I tell you this story in its somewhat macabre humor as an illustration of denial. Going to a festive dinner that night was very different from our Christmas celebration years later. One was honest, somber, and present both to the reality of the day and the reality of eternity, and the other was numbing and dishonoring, increasing our sorrow by diminishing it. We don't want to live in denial. We want to embrace defiant joy.

The evening after my mother's passing was simply not a time for cheering; it was a time for weeping. It was a time to allow our hearts the quiet, the rest, and the repose they needed to begin to absorb the loss. Beauty would have helped. A quiet walk in the woods or along the shore would have been good. But instead we got blades, flames, and suppression of the sorrow filling our hearts. Trying to diminish the pain only increased its potency.

Ignoring reality does not breed joy. Pretending that what is true does not exist is not holy defiance. The seeds of joy can only be firmly planted in the pungent soil of the here and now while at the same time being tethered to eternity. Joy is fully rooted in the truth. Joy embraces all the senses and is fully awake to the laughter, the wonder, and the beauty present in the moment as well as the sorrow, the angst, and the fear. Joy says, "Even so, I have a reason to celebrate."

Crazy, right? Sounds like God. A God who laughs at the sneers of the enemy, stares suffering in the face, and proclaims with fierce love, "You do not have the final word." And as He does, He captures our deep hearts with a hope that defies death.

Defiant may not be a word we would normally associate with the living God, but it can actually be quite fitting. Defiance means resistance, opposition, noncompliance, disobedience, dissent, and rebellion. And when it comes to things that would destroy our souls, that is exactly the right response.

We are called to resist the lies of the enemy. Like Christian in *Pilgrim's Progress*, we do not comply with the Vanity Fair offerings of the world. We are instructed not to obey the clamoring of the flesh. We are urged to rebel against sin. By the life of Christ in us, we oppose death and destruction. We dissent by casting our vote against the belief that sorrow and endless suffering win.

Instead we welcome life, love, and the full work of Christ to bring all of His goodness into every aspect of our and His domains. We comply with truth. We obey our God. We respect

His authority and His final say. We overcome evil with good. We defy hatred by embracing love.

We choose joy.

In the midst of all the suffering in the world, it can feel irresponsible, even frivolous, to have joy. And yet, and still, we are called to it. Certainly there is a time to grieve. There is a time to mourn. To wail. To sigh. There is a time to know our loss and not have to cheer the teppanyaki chef, but that doesn't mean we can't have joy even in that painful knowing. Joy is the heartbeat of the kingdom of God. Joy is what sustains us; it is our strength. We can be resilient. We can be filled with the expectation of good things.

And we can have joy in the midst of the lamentations of our lives.

Joy, Not Happiness

What exactly does it mean, though, to have joy? I think we know instinctively that joy is different from happiness. Both are great. But joy seems higher, doesn't it? Better somehow. Rooted in more reliable things.

Happiness is circumstantial. I'm happy when I wake up and realize it's not Monday but Saturday—I have a day off! I'm happy when someone brings me a cup of coffee. I'm happy when I get a birthday card. I'm sad when a vacation is over. I'm sad when I mishandle the heart of a friend. I'm sad when no one remembers my birthday.

I love being happy. But happiness is unpredictable; it feels vulnerable because it is tied to my circumstances. And don't we all know it. One day you're up; next day you're down. Circumstantial happiness is an emotional roller coaster; it can really take you for a ride. It makes us heartsick in the way rolling seas and careening decks make us seasick.

Joy is something else altogether. It feels firmer, richer, less vulnerable somehow. I'm happy when my family goes out for ice cream, but it seems a little overblown to say I was filled with joy because of it. I was joyful the weddings of my three sons. I was filled with joy over the birth of our granddaughters. Joy flooded my heart when a dear friend was cleared of cancer. I don't think it was merely happiness; the joy felt rooted in the presence of God. His hand was so evident.

Joy is *not* happiness on steroids. It is not happiness squared. Every healthy human being has the capacity to feel happiness, but joy is something entirely different, made up of its own unique substance. It doesn't come with the price of admission. Joy is connected to God and reserved for those who are tapping into His reservoir, who are connected to His life.

Joy is rooted in God and His kingdom, in the surety of His goodness, His love for us. It is immovable. Unshakable. Joy is available at all times, day and night, because God and His kingdom are always available to us. I'm ready to get off the roller coaster of happiness; I want my heart grounded in the higher place of joy. I bet you do too.

Who among us does not want more joy in our lives? In

our work. In our marriages. In our relationships. With our children. In our quiet moments alone. If joy is a fruit of the Spirit (and it is), then we are meant to experience and enjoy it, regardless of our circumstances. Whatever may be swirling around us, the eye of the storm is joy. But how do we get there? The simple answer is we need to come to know God more deeply. When we do, we can believe and rest in His faithful, immovable, immeasurable love for us in every moment we are in.

Joy *is* the heartbeat of heaven, the very light that emanates from Jesus' heart, so as we grow closer in relationship with God, we'll also grow in joy. We'll see that He is not spending His moments wringing His hands, as we are sometimes prone to do. He is not braced against the future or overcome by serious hardship. His joy is never up for grabs. Rather, His joy is immovable, just as He is. It is an essential part of His very person.

Thirteenth-century mystic and poet Meister Eckhart wrote:

Do you want to know what goes on in the heart of the Trinity?

I will tell you.

In the heart of the Trinity the Father laughs and gives birth to the Son.

The Son laughs back at the Father and gives birth to the Spirit.

The whole Trinity laughs and gives birth to us.

We are born from the laughter of the Trinity. What an amazing thought. As image bearers of the Living God, surely joy is written deep in our very hearts. So it should come naturally, right?

Time for a confession. I am not a naturally joyful person. My battle in life has not been needing to be pulled back into reality because of my Pollyanna worldview. My battle has been with depression, ranging from debilitating to a mental-health low-grade fever, the struggle to get out of bed in the morning is one I am acquainted with. I know what it feels like to spend your days walking through sludge up to your knees with a heavy cloak on your back. But I also know the incredible feeling of having it replaced with a sense of hope and promise leading to a deep, untouchable joy. I'm learning. I do want to get off the emotional roller coaster of circumstantial happiness. I do want to be rooted and grounded in joy. Sometimes, though, it takes more intentionality to pursue it in our lives. Sometimes it's hard to take hold of. But it's worth it.

That's what I'm after. That's what I believe God is calling us to. It's what I am calling us to as well.